Social Architecture

Building On-line Communities

Social Architecture

Building On-line Communities

Pieter Hintjens

For my friends

Social Architecture

Published by Pieter Hintjens

Cover font: Kontrapunkt by Bo Linnemann, Kontrapunkt A/S. Text fonts: EB Garamond by Georg Duffner, Mono-space Typewriter by Manfred Klein.

ISBN 978-1533112453

Pieter Hintjens is a programmer, writer, and thinker who has founded many on-line communities. In 2005 he led the European fight against software patents, helping thousands of activists to organize on-line. In 2007 he founded the successful and broad-ranging ZeroMQ community.

Other books by the same author: "ZeroMQ - Messaging for Many Applications" (O'Reilly), "Culture and Empire: Digital Revolution" (Amazon.com), "The Psychopath Code" (Amazon.com).

Contents

Preface

The Wisdom of Crowds

Niccolo Machiavelli observed, in "*Discourses on the First Decade of Titus Livius*" that:

> "*As for prudence and stability of purpose, I affirm that a people is more prudent, more stable, and of better judgment than a prince. Nor is it without reason that the voice of the people has been likened to the voice of God; for we see that wide-spread beliefs fulfill themselves, and bring about marvelous results.*"

In his book "The Wisdom of Crowds," James Surowiecki wrote, "*under the right circumstances, groups are remarkably intelligent, and are often smarter than the smartest people in them.*" He noted that a collective intelligence usually produces better outcomes than a small group of experts, even if members of the crowd do not know all the facts or choose, individually, to act irrationally.

To put it another way, a group of random people will on average be smarter than a few experts. It's a counterintuitive thesis that mocks centuries of received wisdom. Experts in the field of human intelligence (sociologists, anthropologists, psychologists) did not embrace Surowiecki's opinions. He went further: adding more experts to an expert group will make it stupider, while adding laymen could make a stupid group smarter again. Like any recipe, it only works in specific circumstances.

I discovered Surowiecki when I started working on a reproducible recipe for building communities. His work immediately resonated with what I'd experienced, and it seemed testable. I had both the opportunity to apply it, and to experiment with enough communities to try to disprove it: the basis, thus, for real science.

Out of that work came a process for building smart, self-guiding, successful on-line communities that could beat expert groups every time. It is a discipline I named *Social Architecture*, which for a while let me call myself a "Social Architect." (Today, I'm a struggling writer, which sounds more romantic.)

Social Architecture, by analogy with conventional architecture, is the process and the product of planning, designing, and growing an on-line community. Social Architectures in the form of on-line communities are the cultural and political symbols and works of art of digital society. The twenty-first century will be identified with its surviving Social Architectures.

As Social Architects, we participate in communities, we identify successful naturally occurring patterns or develop new patterns (which I call "tools"), and we apply these deliberately to our own projects. We apply psychology (our social instincts), economics (how we create common wealth through specialization and trade), politics (how we collect and share power), and technology (how we communicate). We continually adapt our toolkit based on new knowledge and experience. Our goal is to create on-line communities that can and do accurately solve the problems we identify, grow healthily, and survive on their own.

Successful on-line communities tend to be based on the contract of mutual benefit, whether implicit or explicit. That is, it is possible to build a billion dollar business based on volunteer labor, with every participant contributing for selfish reasons. Often, participants do not realize or care that they are part of a community. However, every action we take is economic. "Crowd sourcing" is the exploitation for profit of volunteer labor. And it only works when the crowd really wants to solve the problems you throw at it, or the ones it discovers.

Wiser and More Constant than a Prince

Machiavelli didn't explain or provide evidence for his observation. However the understanding that the collective will is accurate and honest — *vox populi, vox Dei* — pervades modern culture. It underpins our sometimes skeptical appreciation of democracy, and it justifies our demands for transparency and access to information. It is the basis for modern economies, based on free choice and free markets.

Surowiecki identified four elements necessary for a wise crowd[1]: diversity of opinion, independence of members from one another, decentralization, and effective ways to aggregate opinions. He describes the ideal wise crowd as consisting of many independently minded individuals who are loosely connected, who are geographically and socially diverse, who are unemotional about their subject, who each have many sources of information, and who have some way to bring their individual judgments together into a collective decision.

According to Surowiecki, the wise crowd makes fast and accurate judgments, organizes itself to make the best use of resources, and cooperates without central authority. Some examples of wise crowds, such as Wikipedia, are extraordinarily successful despite intense and repeated criticism from naysayers and attacks from vandals and infiltrators. It's such a compelling proposition that we might wonder why we don't see more wise crowds. Indeed, why is the world filled with so much stupidity if it's so easy to be smart?

There are good explanations for the stupidity of many crowds, and I'll explore this in detail in my book "Culture & Empire", from which this section is drawn. Few people have tried to explain group stupidity in terms of collective wisdom. And without a clear understanding of function, how can we hope to understand dysfunction?

So the apparent failure of collective intelligence convinces many that this is just a fancy theory that fails in practice. And yet if we look at on-line communities, for example those that form around popular open source software projects like my company ZeroMQ[2], we see groups that look a lot like Surowiecki's wise crowds. While it may be hard to spot wise crowds in the physical world, they seem to be the

1   https://en.wikipedia.org/wiki/Wisdom_of_crowds
2   http://zeromq.org

dominant model on line. Through trial and error, digital society has rediscovered the principles of wise crowds and adopted them as its core operating principles.

Digital society's solution to the ancient problem of corrupt authority is elegant and successful. There are literally millions of communities, each backed by the authority of its founders. Citizens of digital society choose freely which authorities to respect and which to ignore. The core trick is to accept authority without giving it the "right to command."

Thus there is intense competition to develop fair authority that does not command, and instead enforces necessary rules. It is a deeply subversive truth. Generations that learn this model will refuse — to the point of death — to respect industrial society's model — enforced by iron curtains and armed border guards if needed — where the citizen literally belongs to the State.

Origins of Social Architecture

I've bet a lot of money on Social Architecture, and have made good profits. It comes close to hard social science, proven by years of reproducible experiments on living cases and studies of existing communities. It mixes psychology, economics, politics, technology, humanism, and optimism into something that I've found can make a lot of people pretty happy.

My journey into Social Architecture began in the late 1990's, when I began researching a book about how cults exploit our social instincts. Cults are not happy places, of course. However, humans are drawn to them because we're social animals who, over the last million years, have developed instincts for joining and conforming to groups in order to survive. It has become second nature for us to readily respect authority, conform, learn common languages, and adopt shared behavior. Cult groups brainwash their members by exploiting these instincts. They separate members from their families, eliminate privacy, flood them with jargon, create arbitrary rules, and punish and reward randomly.

In this way, cults can turn most ordinary people into unthinking followers who willingly empty their bank accounts, steal from their families, and work for years without pay. As a student watching the occasional friend disappear into the caverns of Scientology and other cults, this struck me as malignant and confusing. Later, when my closest cousin dropped out and lost five years of his life to Scientology, it got personal.

Studying the Cult Information Centre (CIC) website[3], it struck me that these brainwashing techniques all have several things in common. First, they were all clearly focused on attacking individual thought and action, and destroying that which makes us strong. Second, they were reminiscent of environments in which I'd worked (big business often functions like a cult). Third, they all seemed reversible in that they could be flipped around to become positive patterns.

The last aspect is surprising. If a hammer breaks a window, you can hardly make a window stronger by reversing the hammer. Some examples make it clear. Take this technique from the CIC site: "*Peer Group Pressure — Suppressing doubt and resistance to new ideas by exploiting the need to belong.*" The reverse is, by lowering the cost of joining and leaving the group, we encourage new ideas and criticism. Or, consider "*Removal of Privacy — Achieving loss of ability to evaluate logically by preventing private contemplation.*" Its reverse is: give people private space and time to think, and they'll become better at thinking logically.

My conclusions persist. We survive by attaching to groups, following others, and trying to make sense of the world. Some groups work by domesticating and brutalizing us. Other groups work by giving us freedom and allowing us to be stronger, smarter, and more independent.

---

3   http://www.cultinformation.org.uk/question_what-is-mind-control.html

In 2000, the Internet had not yet become cheap enough for mass-market use, and open source communities were small and often regional, frequently focused around universities. Open source communities such as the Debian Foundation[4] still operated as classic not-for-profit organizations, as legal entities with boards, treasurers, and the like.

In 2005, I joined a number of collaborative projects. On the one hand, I was involved with the FFII[5], working to stop software patents in Europe. We (the good guys) spoke in the European Parliament, debated with the European Patent Office (the bad guys), organized seminars, tabled amendments, got votes, and broadly, took part in the largest lobbying effort ever to hit Brussels.

On the other hand, I was developing open standards, starting with the Advanced Message Queuing Protocol (AMQP). The contrast between the cultures of these organizations was sharp. The FFII was a group of crazy volunteers, creative beyond belief, and filled with hard cold determination to stop SAP, Siemens, Microsoft, and Nokia (more bad guys) from changing European law to legalize the gray market in patents on software. The AMQP workgroup included banks and large software firms, who turned out to be crazy in a different and less enjoyable way.

With insanity surrounding me on all sides, research on social instincts and cult techniques suddenly seemed relevant again. With my friends in the FFII, we launched campaign after campaign. Websites, petitions, email lists, conferences ... it never stopped. Most of our campaigns failed to get any real scale though a few did. Above all, for about three years, we experimented, and we collected results.

We learned two broad things. First, a cult is the flipside of a wise crowd. The cult patterns seemed accurate, and I watched people applying the cult model to others over and over. Any intense group, family, business, or team starts to resemble a cult, in little or larger

4   http://www.debian.org/doc/manuals/project-history/ch-detailed.en.html
5   http://ffii.org

ways. It's a matter of degree. However, as soon as you spend your free time on someone else's project, you are essentially starting to slide down that slope. I watched as entire groups went off the rails, unable to think straight or produce accurate results. There was a straight causal effect: as the group became more cult-like, they became more useless.

The second thing is that just reversing the cult techniques isn't enough. It does make a good start to promote individual strength and creativity, yet that is not the same as building a solid community. For that, you need more explicit patterns. Define a powerful mission to attract newcomers. Make it really easy for people to get involved. Embrace argument and conflict; it's where good ideas come from. Delegate systematically, and create competition. Work with volunteers more than employees. Get diversity and scale. Make people own the work; don't let the work own the people.

It is of course much cheaper and faster to do large-scale experiments with people on line than in the real world. To prove or disprove a recipe for building a community, all you have to do is create a space, define some rules for play, announce it to the world, and sit back and watch.

My largest and most successful experiment to date, which I'll refer to often in this chapter, is the ZeroMQ software community[6]. It has grown from a team in a Slovak cellar to a global community, and is used by thousands of organizations. Above all, ZeroMQ is entirely built and steered by its community: over a hundred contributors to the core library, and a hundred other projects around that.

---

6   http://zeromq.org

Chapter 1. The Toolbox

In my Social Architect's toolbox, I have 20 tools, each covering one aspect of a community or group. These tools work in two ways. First, you can use them to measure an existing community, giving a rating of zero or more. Second, you can use them when you design a community, to help you focus your effort on where it will be most useful.

- *Strong mission* — the stated reason for the group's existence
- *Free entry* — how easy it is for people to join the group
- *Transparency* — how openly and publicly decisions are made
- *Free contributors* — how far people are paid to contribute
- *Full remixability* — how far contributors can remix each others' work
- *Strong protocols* — how well the rules are written
- *Fair authority* — how well the rules are enforced
- *Non-tribalism* — how far the group claims to own its participants
- *Self-organization* — how far individuals can assign their own tasks
- *Tolerance* — how the group embraces conflicts
- *Measurable success* — how well the group can measure its progress
- *High scoring* — how the group rewards its participants
- *Decentralization* — how widely the group is spread out
- *Free workspaces* — how easy it is to create new projects
- *Smooth learning* — how easy it is to get started and keep learning
- *Regular structure* — how regular and predictable the overall structure is
- *Positivity* — how far the group is driven by positive goals
- *Sense of humor* — how seriously the group takes itself
- *Minimalism* — how much excess work the group does

- *Sane funding* — how the group survives economically

We will look at these tools one by one and see how they work in various communities. First, some general advice about building a community. Be brutally honest with yourself and with others. Your biggest challenge is overcoming your own prejudices and biases, and then those of everyone you work with.

Whatever toolkit I can provide you with, you'll want to adapt and extend it for your own needs. Social Architecture is still a very young science and many of my tools will be too complex, or incomplete. Here's the best way I know to do that:

- *Consume your own product.* If you are not a fanatical user of whatever your group is making, you are half-blind. I learned this when working for Nigerian Breweries in the 1990's: by enjoying beer, I learned to appreciate the business of selling beer so much better.

- *Practice and repeat.* It is cheap to experiment, and failure is healthy. By definition, if you start a project and it fails, no one notices. So start many projects and change or fix your tools if they don't work.

- *Do first-line support.* All communities have a place where newcomers arrive and ask questions. Be there, observe how new visitors get lost, what mistakes they make, and improve your designs accordingly. Perhaps the mission confuses them. Or maybe the structures are confusing. A good designer sympathizes with his users, feels their pain, and works to relieve it.

- *Release early, release often.* This is a mantra from free software communities. It's accurate. You want to do your design work in the open, and get critical feedback as early as possible. In ZeroMQ, we release every patch as it happens.

- *Learn and teach all the time.* Teaching gives you perspective, and learning lets you pick up new tools over time. Social Architecture is a young craft, and though the basics are solidly anchored in human psychology, there are still many unknowns.

Strong Mission

The starting point for any community is a stated mission. The mission defines the goals that we can all agree on in advance, before we join the project. It's like the title of a website or the slogan for a movie. For instance, Reddit's title is: "the front page of the Internet," an ambitious mission that it nonetheless achieved. Facebook's slogan is: "helps you connect and share with the people in your life."

TIP: Use your mission as a slogan, on your website, marketing, presentations, and so on. If you are investing money in your community, you may want to trademark the mission statement.

Without a clear mission, an on-line community won't grow. A group of friends who start a project may agree what they want to do, yet anyone new coming on board has to guess what they had in mind. People will guess wrong, and will change their minds over time. This leads to confusion, disagreement, and disappointment as people find that their hard work was wasted because the rest of the group headed off in a different direction.

A good mission saunters past "sane" and steps into "you cannot be serious!" Wikipedia's mission, "the free encyclopedia that anyone can edit"[7] is a good example. It was, initially, a goal that everyone, except a few idealists, found impossible and crazy. Those idealists were precisely who Wikipedia needed to get on board on day one. Impossible missions attract the right kind of people for a young project.

TIP: Change your mission as your community matures. At first, you will want to attract idealists and pioneers, then the leading edge, and then early adopters, the mass market, and finally, the late adopters. Each of these groups wants different things. Understand that, and tune your mission to suit.

To formulate a good mission, think in terms of the single main problem your project is solving. Reddit, for instance, is solving the problem of how to get the news off an Internet with far too many in-

---

7   https://en.wikipedia.org/wiki/Main_Page

teresting sources of information. Its "front page" represents the digit-al newspaper of the twenty-first century. Wikipedia is solving the problem of how to collect knowledge from the minds of billions. "Anyone can edit" represents *vox populi, vox Dei*, the understanding that truth, if it exists, comes only from the minds of many.

TIP: When proposing action, small or large, try always to start by identifying the problems you want to solve. Only when you have a clear and real problem on which everyone can agree, move to discuss-ing solutions. A solution for an assumed problem is like a group without a clear mission.

You may have multiple missions, by accident or deliberately. This can be traumatic if the missions pull in different directions. For ex-ample, growing a group larger may require subsidies, which conflicts with making profits. If Wikipedia became a for-profit entity with ad-vertising and an expensive tranche of managers, do you think its com-munity would grow or shrink?

For ZeroMQ, our stated mission was "Fastest. Messaging. Ever." This is a nice, and nearly impossible answer to a problem we could all agree on: namely, the slow, bloated technology available at that time. However, my co-founder Martin and I had conflicting goals. He wanted to build the best software possible, while I wanted to build the largest community possible. As the user base grew, his dramatic changes, which broke existing applications, caused increasing pain.

In that case, we were able to make everyone happy (Martin went off to build a new library called "Nano"). However if you cannot resolve mission conflicts, it can damage the project severely. Projects can sur-vive a lot of arguments, however fights between founders are traumat-ic.

TIP: If the founders agree that "success" is defined as "having the most participants possible," it can help in keeping your focus over the years. It also makes it easy to measure your success as you grow.

Free Entry

Once you have agreed on your mission, you need to test this against the real world. That is, you have to make a minimal yet plausible answer to the problem you identified. I call this a "seed." With the seed, you have two main goals. First, to start to collect idealists and pioneers (basically, anyone mad enough to trust you) into a community. Second, to prove or disprove your mission.

Projects fail for many reasons. A major cause of failure is that the original idea or mission wasn't as amazing as people felt. Failure is fine, even excellent, unless it costs years of your life. Making a seed and showing it to a few people isn't enough because most people won't be really critical. They feel it's hurtful. However, ask people to invest even a few hours of their time in making it better, and if they don't say "yes," you know how they really feel.

TIP: Build a "seed" product in public view and encourage others to get involved from the start. If people do get involved, promote them rapidly. If they don't, treat that as a sign your mission may be wrong. Use the seed product to build the community.

Once people agree to help you, they need somewhere to work together. You need a "collaboration platform." My two favorites are Wikidot[8] for knowledge communities, and GitHub[9] for software projects. The platform has to be free to use. It has to be easy to learn and work with. Your seed project has to be visible to anonymous visitors. It has to work for anyone no matter his or her age, gender, education, or physical location.

All this makes it possible for interesting strangers to walk up and look at your work and, if they like it and feel challenged by it, get involved little by little. You want to be working on your seed in public view, and talking about your new project, from the very start. This means people can make suggestions, and feel involved, from day one.

---

8   http://wikidot.com
9   http://github.com

If we, as founders of a group, choose those we work with, we're building in "selection bias." It is much easier to work with those nice, smart people who agree with us, than the idiots and critics who disagree. And when you agree with me, you just confirm all of my biases and assumptions and I know from experience that those can be wrong in the most amazing ways.

Over time, collecting people who share the same broken assumptions and biases can kill a project. For example, when making software protocols, the requirements for large firms can be very different from those for small open source teams. So if a protocol committee is built entirely out of large firms, what they make will be indigestible by the mass of the market.

The answer is free entry to anyone who is interested, no matter how different or apparently crazy their perspectives. This gives us, potentially, that broad and diverse community which is the raw material for a wise crowd. In ZeroMQ, we never turn away anyone who wants to contribute. I pull people in, even if their contributions are poor or incorrect. The community is more important than the product.

When the community has matured around the seed product, they will want to build a second generation of it. As Social Architect, your goal is to time and guide this properly so that you can use the wise crowd to help design the "real" product. It's possible that around this point you will want to find a good domain name and make a "proper" website.

TIP: If people are not joining in your seed, don't continue working on it. Instead, discover what's stopping them from joining and fix that. Start again from scratch if necessary. Don't prematurely kill seeds; it can take time for people to appreciate what you are trying to do.

Transparency

Transparency is very important to get rapid criticism of ideas and work in progress. If a few people in a team go off and work on something together for some time — a few days seems harmless, a few weeks is not — then what they make can be presented to the group as a *fait accompli*. When one person does that, the group can just shrug it off. When two or more people do that, it becomes much harder to back off from bad ideas. Secrecy and incompetence seem bound together. Groups that work in secret do not achieve wisdom.

TIP: When one person does something in a dark corner, that's an experiment. When two or more people do something in a dark corner, that's a conspiracy.

With ZeroMQ, it took us some years to come to a really open and transparent situation. Before that, the core contributors mostly worked in secret, publishing their work when they felt it was ready for public view. By the time they did that, it was very hard for the rest of the community to say "no." And often the work was off course, a brilliant solution to a problem no one really cared about. In the end, we explicitly banned this kind of thing.

It is ironic that secrets seem essential to certain business models. Profits often come from the ignorance of customers. Most profit-making businesses, even large communities like Twitter, depend on a strict division between "them" and "us." However, digital society grows best by putting scale before profits, and by treating all ignorance as a problem to solve. If your clients are ignorant of your internal thought processes, then you will be ignorant of where those processes are wrong.

Free Contributors

Money is a funny thing. Too little, and the community starves (I'll return to this later). Too much, and it rots. It is important to understand why each contributor is there at all. *What are their economic motives?* Even in a volunteer community, every person is there for self-interested reasons.

In ZeroMQ, we originally started with a small paid team and moved after two years to a community of volunteers through the pragmatic — if not very gentle — tactic of running out of money and having to fire the developers. A few disappeared to other jobs, some came back as contributors, and the project became more exciting and fun than before. People contribute to ZeroMQ because they need it in their own projects, and if they spend a little time making it better, that can earn them or save them many times more.

When you work for someone else, you will make what he or she wants. When you work for yourself, you will make what you need. It is so very different. People with money yet no skill or taste are the rif-fraff of society. We despise paid contributors to Wikipedia, paid blog-gers, and paid moderators on Reddit, because we know that the opin-ions they express are almost by definition false. Would a blogger paid by Hollywood criticize the new summer blockbuster?

I've nothing against employees. However, if you are aiming for the largest, most successful community, you want contributors who are there for honest, transparent reasons. If a filmmaker comes to Reddit to discuss his work, that is fantastic. If his marketing staff come to downvote critical comments, that is despicable.

TIP: One free contributor is worth 10 paid contributors.

Full Remixability

A group needs a lot of agreements for working together. I call these "protocols." Perhaps the most important one for any creative com-munity is remixability. Whether it's music, art, images, video, com-ments, software, or wiki pages, the following question *will* arise: "What is the copyright license on this work, and how does that affect the community?"

Broadly, there are three types of agreement for copyright:

1. A "locked down" license that does not allow remixing. This is the old way of working, and still the dominant model in for-profit work.

2. A "free to take" license that allows one-way remixing. This is the dominant model for many open source software communities.

3. A "share-alike" license that enforces two-way remixing. This is the dominant model for free software communities like ZeroMQ, and for many artistic communities (though it may be an unwritten agreement).

Users prefer the "free to take" model because it lets them use the content in any way they like without reciprocity. Imagine a DJ who releases a popular track under the "free to take" model. Then a company makes a remix and uses that for an advert. And that remix will be locked down. Now, the DJ cannot remix that new work, and may find himself unable even to play the remix.

Communities, however, work better with the third model because it converts users into contributors. With a share-alike license, the DJ would be able to take the remix, mix that further, and turn it into a dance club success. Knowledge and ideas flow in all directions, rather than leaking out of the community into closed dead-ends. The shift is powerful, especially for those of us building communities with a minimal budget. If you're a large firm putting a lot of money into a community, the "free to take" model can work better.

TIP: If every contributor owns their specific contributions, and you use a share-alike license, you don't need copyright assignments or re-licensing from contributors.

Strong Protocols

Good protocols let strangers collaborate without up-front agreement. They resolve destructive conflict, and turn it into valuable competition. The insight that lets anarchists join wise crowds as happily as anyone is that the crowd can develop its own rules. Typically, these rules govern remixing, identity, ranking, and so on. No matter what their form, good rules are simple, clear, explicitly written down, and agreed upon by all.

If you're building a software project, you might take an existing rulebook, like the C4 protocol[10] we built for ZeroMQ. Otherwise,

---

10   http://rfc.zeromq.org/spec:2

you can start with a minimal rulebook and grow it over time as you see what problems hit the community. This is, for example, how the Wikipedia rulebook[11] grew up.

Some rules must be established very early (such as licenses for con‐tributions). Others can be developed when needed (such as processes for resolving conflicts). Complex, pointless, or unwritten rules are toxic to groups. They create space for argument, confuse people, and make it expensive to join or leave a group.

TIP: Write your rules very carefully, starting with choosing a li‐cense for content, and measure how much they help people. Change them over time as you need to.

Fair Authority

Without authority, rules have no strength. The community founders and main contributors are its de facto authority. If they ab‐use this position, they lose contributors and the project dies or gets forked under different rules. Authority needs to be scalable (that is, work with any size of group) and transferable as the group grows and changes over time.

While we need authority to build a flat playing field, many groups use authority as a way of controlling members, keeping them in the group, and making them conform. A favorite cult technique is to ran‐domly punish and reward people so they become confused and stop questioning authority.

TIP: Promote the most active contributors into positions of au‐thority, and do this rapidly. You have a short window for promoting new contributors before they disappear to other projects.

You have to be a part of your community, and you must follow your own rules. If you find yourself breaking, or wanting to break, your own rules, they are faulty and need fixing.

---

11   http://simple.wikipedia.org/wiki/Wikipedia:Rules

In the ZeroMQ community, we've had fights over who had the right to define the rules, and in the end it came to the trademark and domain name. The person or company who owns the project name is the ultimate authority for the rules. If they're nuts, the project will die.

TIP: If you are investing money in the community, then consider taking a US trademark so that you can stop people from making similarly-named imitations that don't follow your processes. It costs about $750.

Non-Tribalism

Membership must be a badge to collect, not an identity. As Mr. Spock so often observed, emotions are not logical. Some groups are driven by logical purpose, and others by more emotional factors such as peer pressure, the herd instinct, and even collective hysteria. The main factor seems to be the relationship between the group and its members. We can quantify this: *Do members "belong exclusively" to the group?* Exclusive membership means putting the group's existence above its work. Exclusive membership ends in conflict with other groups.

TIP: Stay away from formal membership models, especially those that try to convert people to belonging to the group. Allow anonymous or unidentified participation. Encourage people to create their own competing projects as spaces to experiment and learn.

Industrial-age groups, like cults, specialize in owning their members. An employee belongs to his or her company. In some cases, even ideas you have in the shower are property of your employer. And when a group owns its members, it motivates them with emotions like fear, hate, jealousy, and anger, instead of purposeful logic. The threat of expulsion is widely used to get people to conform. "Do what I say or I'll fire you!"

TIP: To measure how tribal a group is, just start a competing pro-ject. If the response is negative and emotional, the group is tribal. A sane group will applaud its new competitors.

Self-Organization

Some people like to be told what to do. The best contributors and teams choose their own tasks. A successful community recognizes problems and organizes itself to solve them. Further, it does that faster and more accurately than any top-down management structure. This means the community should accept contributions in any area, without limit.

Top-down task assignment is an anti-pattern with many weak-nesses. It makes it impossible for individuals to act when they recog-nize new problems. It creates fiefdoms where work and the necessary resources belong to specific people. It creates long communication chains that can't react rapidly. It requires layers of managers just to connect decision-makers with those doing the work.

TIP: Write rules to raise the quality of work and to explicitly allow anyone to work on anything they find interesting.

In ZeroMQ, we removed all assigned tasks from the community. For example, we don't accept feature requests. If someone wants a feature, they either send us a patch, or offer someone money to make the change, or they wait. This means people only make changes they really need to make.

TIP: Communities need power hierarchies. However, they should be fluid and heavily delegated. That is, choose the people you work with, and let them choose the people they work with. Power struc-tures are like liquid cement; they harden and stop people from mov-ing around as they need to. Any structure defends itself.

Tolerance

A diverse group has conflicting opinions, and a healthy group has to embrace and digest these conflicts. Critics, iconoclasts, vandals, spies, and trolls keep a group on its toes. They can be a catalyst for others to stay involved. Wikipedia thrives thanks to, not in spite of, those who click Edit to make a mess of articles.

It's a classic anti-pattern to suppress minority ideas and views on the basis that they are "dangerous." This inevitably means suppressing new ideas as well. The logic is usually that group coherence is more important than diversity. What then happens is that mistakes aren't challenged, and get solidified into policy. In fact, the group can be more important than the results, if it is diverse and open to arguments. This is a difficult lesson that applies to broad society as well: there are no dangerous opinions, only dangerous responses.

The way communities deal with trolls and vandals is one thing. To deal with fundamental differences in viewpoint is something else. I've said before that conflicting missions can be a problem. The best answer I know is to turn the conflict into competition.

In software, we do this by making standards that teams can build on. Take for example the HTTP standard that powers the web. Any team can build a web server or a web browser. This lets teams compete. So Google's Chrome browser emerged as a lightweight, faster alternative to Firefox, which was getting bloated and slow. Then, the Firefox team took performance seriously, and now Firefox is faster than Chrome.

TIP: When there is an interesting problem, try to get multiple teams competing to solve it. Competition is great fun and can produce better answers than monopolized problems. You can even explicitly create competitions with prizes for the best solutions.

Measurable Success

It's all very well to try to turn conflict into competition. However, you also need to provide teams with a way to know how well they are doing. The best tools, like GitHub, show you precisely how many people are watching or have "starred" or "forked" a particular project (revealing different levels of interest and commitment).

The Web, of course, has always been obsessed with "hits" and traffic analysis, which show exactly how popular a specific site or page is. This makes it very easy to measure success of on-line projects. In the old industrial-era business, teams get their feedback from their bosses. This turns into an exercise in power: you'll be scored higher for compliance than for accuracy. Making your bosses happy so they give you a pay raise is not healthy.

TIP: If your platform does not support it directly, find ways to tell contributors how well their projects are doing.

High Scoring

There are many reasons why people contribute to communities. An overriding motivation is to be admired for success. That can be as an individual, or as part of a team. Success is relative so we need metrics, some high score that people can see and track.

In the ZeroMQ community, we don't emphasize high scoring much, though contributors do get more love when they contribute more. It goes on their permanent record. Contributing to ZeroMQ can land you a good job.

Reddit, like many sites, uses "karma" that shows how many votes a profile got for its posts and submissions. It works pretty well. Some sites don't show all karma in order to stop people playing the system to just get a higher score. Some sites, like StackOverflow, have taken "gamification" to an extreme level, with badges, high scores, achievements, and so on. I think this is manipulative and distorts the mission of the community. People should be contributing because they need the project to succeed, not to earn toy points.

Having said that, social credit — making groups of strangers happy — is enormously satisfying and does not pollute the planet. Industrial society focuses on material rewards (higher salary, larger house, nicer car) tied into a hierarchical structure. It is effective because we all like wealth, or we have a daddy complex; whatever the reason, wanting to make the boss happy means taking fewer risks.

TIP: When there is something that people are asking for, and you don't know how to do it yourself, announce publicly that it is "impossible." Or, propose a solution that is so awkward and hopeless that it annoys real experts into stepping up.

Decentralization

In his book, Surowiecki explained how the Columbia Space Shuttle disaster was caused by a hierarchical NASA management bureaucracy that ignored the knowledge of low-level engineers. If a group is decentralized, its members are more independent, they receive more diverse inputs, and they are also likely to be more diverse from the start.

If a group is geographically concentrated, it becomes homogenized, where all members get pretty much the same inputs and triggers. Close proximity also lets a minority dominate the mindset of the group and quash unorthodox ideas. It lets them literally bully or bluff the majority into compliance. Insisting that all members of a group sit in the same office, department, or building is an old anti-pattern that is hard to break. There's a reason cults have compounds.

TIP: Do you need meetings to get work done as a group? This is a sign that you have deeper problems in how you work together. You are excluding people who are not physically close by.

It can be hard to move away from the old discuss-then-execute model of working together. Certainly it's easier if you are building groups from scratch than if you are trying to change existing groups.

Free Workspaces

A community needs space in which to grow. In Internet terms, this is typically a website or collection of sites, and related structures like email lists, blogs, and so on. We've seen that it's become very cheap, or free, to create "space" in digital society. The question is, can individuals create their own spaces within the community? If so, they will invest more in the collective project.

The freedom to create structure annoys people who feel that it creates chaos and disorder. However, if you use regular structures (see the next section), there's no real cost to participants. What is toxic is *speculatively* creating structure based on the assumption that people might need it. When I took charge of the FFII association in 2005, the previous president had created several hundred email lists, representing all the projects *he* felt people should be working on. It didn't fit how people wanted to organize, and it was very hard to delete these lists and create the ones we actually needed.

Of course, industrial-era groups do assign work, and assign the resources to carry it out. Any new infrastructure — such as a website, email list, or wiki — requires approval and a decision. It might even need legal review due to copyright and patent concerns. The cost is high, so people are reluctant to take the risk. Thus, they don't experiment and often work with one hand tied behind their backs.

In the ZeroMQ software community, it takes a single click to create a new project. In Wikipedia, you can create a new page simply by clicking "create this page." Both projects have mechanisms to stop random garbage from accumulating. Wikipedia purges new pages quite aggressively. ZeroMQ has an extra manual step to bring a new project into the official community organization.

TIP: Make it absolutely simple for logged-in users to create new projects. If projects are organized per user, you don't need to worry about junk. If they're in a shared space, you may need tools to purge junk and abandoned projects.

Regular Structure

As a community grows larger, it can become harder to navigate. If you make a single, ever-growing project, this becomes more and more complex over time, consisting mainly of special cases. Think of a medieval castle. This problem is particularly bad in projects built by larger firms that seem to lack a sense of cost.

Complexity turns people away because it's so difficult to learn. The solution is to use very regular structures that you can learn once and then predict many times. Not any structure will do. We seem bad at learning structures deeper than three or four levels. However, we're happy to explore very wide structures with thousands or millions of boxes if those boxes correspond to separate units of work, or projects. Think of a city.

The successful on-line communities are cities, not castles. Wikipedia consists of a few language-specific wikis, each broken into millions of pages (the projects), each structured into sections, discussion, history, footnotes, and so on. Several people may be working on a page at once, and one person may be slowly editing or caring for dozens or hundreds of pages.

GitHub manages millions of software repositories or "repos," grouped under user profiles or organizations, and each broken into some further structure (source files, documentation, etc.) that usually depends on the language (Java repos use one style, C repos use another, and so on). One repo may have a handful of contributors, and people will work on a few to a dozen repos. The ZeroMQ community consists of an organization that contains a growing number of projects.

TIP: Design your community as a searchable city of projects, where anyone can start a new project, projects represent perhaps a dozen people's work, and all have familiar structure, as much as possible.

Businesses love their castles, which inevitably describe Important People, not projects, and certainly not the major business problems. Their organizations are huge and irregular. There's no way to understand them except by memorizing them in detail. Then again, you can't simply move around the castle, so there's little benefit in learning its layout.

Smooth Learning

When ZeroMQ started, it was one project with a single "README" page. Today, it's a hundred or so smaller projects, each with its own documentation, community, and process. To get into a mature project can be painful. As I've said, regular structures are essential. More than that, you need a fairly specific learning curve that goes from simple to hard as people progress from idle passer-by to expert contributor.

Think of your community as a video game with levels that become increasingly difficult, and have bigger and bigger payoffs. People will play "up to their level." If you can do this right, you attract the most people. If you do this wrong, you'll bore experts by making it too easy, or you'll turn off others by making it too hard to get started.

TIP: Use classic training tools — presentations, videos, answers to frequently asked questions (FAQs), tutorials — to get people started. It helps if you are part of the community so you can see what kinds of questions people ask when they start.

Many existing organizations make no effort to create a smooth curve. Everything starts complex and stays there. To participate, you might need weeks of training. It's inefficient, frustrating, and expensive to scale.

Positivity

It's tempting to try to provoke people into joining a group by being aggressive. After all, many people enjoy a good heated argument, especially when they feel they're right. Some groups thrive on being quite hostile and negative towards other groups, particularly if there is some history involved. The tone you set as founder will last a long time. If you promote your community by attacking competitors, you will attract people of a certain mindset, and the culture will spread. Sooner or later, the negativity will turn inwards and can be very damaging for the community.

TIP: When you talk about people, products, or organizations, be polite and stay balanced. When you promote your product or community, talk about the problems you solve, not how you are better than your competitors.

It's better in my experience to set a positive tone from the start. Competitors are good because they give you resistance. Copycats are good, because they prove your market is a real one. Trolls and vandals are good, because they give sincere people an extra chance to prove their value. And so on. It seems like hard work to look for a positive outcome for every event. However, it's really just a mindset.

TIP: Welcome everyone, and only intervene when there are irredeemable troublemakers. It's a small minority that really can't find a place in an open, diverse community. You can ask such people to leave and, if necessary, ban them.

A positive culture is more tolerant and reduces emotions and arguments. It also makes it easier to experiment, make mistakes, and self-criticize, and all these help a community think through difficult problems.

Sense of Humor

Have you ever wondered why humans have an instinct for humor, and why people who never laugh seem odd or unfriendly? My theory is that we evolved humor as a way of defusing conflict (which has obvious survival value). People don't punch the joker unless the joke is old or badly told. More subtly, humor defuses tribalism and emotion, and lets people work together even when they have huge differences. A shared joke creates strong bonds because it proves the intersection of minds. Humor is an essential part of a community and reduces stress.

TIP: The more serious your message, the more you need humor. In my ZeroMQ book, I wrote a lot of silly nonsense mixed with the heavy technical explanations. Most people enjoyed and appreciated this.

If it weren't for alcohol, the grim-faced industrial economy would barely ever laugh. It takes itself so seriously. The lack of humor in an organization is a sure sign that everyone there is fundamentally miserable. Worse, it makes the group vulnerable to conflict and fracture.

Minimalism

You make a racing car faster by removing weight, not by adding power. You can make your community lighter, faster, and more agile by being dogmatically minimalist about the work you do. Though it sounds lazy, it's often harder to *not* do something that seems fun than to just go ahead and do it.

The general rule is *do the absolute minimum that probably works.* Then invest more only as people start to use your work and complain. Never invest more than the absolute minimum you need to get a "bite" from users. This applies to your seed product as well as every change you make. User feedback — more than your own vision — is the best guide for where to make further investments.

TIP: Perfection precludes participation. Releasing buggy, half-finished work is an excellent way to provoke people into contributing. Though it can be hard for big egos to accept, flaws are usually more attractive to contributors than perfection, which attracts users.

The culture of minimalism can, and should, extend to your community itself. In the past, we used to make legal entities for serious projects so there would be a place to hold copyrights, trademarks, and money. However, legal entities are expensive and time-consuming to manage. Tax reporting by itself can be an unbearable burden.

One of my communities, Digistan[12], was designed, grown, and did its work (building a new generation of legal templates and political arguments for open standards) in about six months. All of our ZeroMQ protocols are based on the Digistan work. The Open Web

---

12   http://www.digistan.org

Foundation[13] — solving the same problem — spent two years simply building a legal entity, defining bylaws, and electing officers.

Sane Funding

If there's not enough money, a community will starve. If there's too much, it will, as I've said, rot. It is a delicate balance. We can motivate people with money up to a certain degree. After that, only sociopaths respond proportionally. This is a flaw in the naive "more money is always good" theory of capitalism. In my business, it's always been those I paid best who turned out to be the most treacherous.

The first thing is to reduce your costs by not setting up legal entities, offices, and staff unless you really need them. Not only will these eat any funding you might have, they will work against you as you try to build a pure on-line community. Secondly, invest your time and money in the community minimally when you see that there's no choice. It could be taking a trademark, paying for hosting services, or doing some particularly difficult work no one else is able to undertake. Finally, watch out for individuals who take on too much risk without adequate reward — they can be vulnerable to burnout, something I'll talk about in the next chapter.

TIP: Every time you find it necessary to spend money on the community, ask if you could have found a way to get others to help instead.

13   https://en.wikipedia.org/wiki/Open_Web_Foundation

Chapter 2. Sidebars

In the previous chapter, I examined my toolbox for building online communities. Now I'll look at few other key ideas that are worth knowing about.

The Market Curve

The market curve[14] is a well-known theory of marketing that is less known in engineering and community building. However it's important to understanding how communities develop over time. In the classic market curve, a new technology, idea, or product enters the market as a wave, starting with ice-breaking enthusiasts and pioneers, then the early adopters, then the mass market, then the late adopters, and finally the skeptics.

Each of these groups has different motivations for coming to a project, joining in, and eventually, leaving. If we take an exciting new technology like ZeroMQ, we can explore this and understand how it works:

- When the project is young and experimental, it attracts pundits and researchers whose business is new stuff, in general. These people need to know why the project is different from what exists, what its goals are, and why it is exciting. They will never use it, nor will they become contributors. They are your evangelists. They often lose interest rapidly.

- When you have a seed product, it attracts pioneers. These are hardcore hackers who want the latest stuff and don't care about documentation, marketing, or tutorials. They're very good at managing the risk of new things. These are your first wave of contributors. Often they are building frameworks for other developers.

---

14   https://www.google.com/search?q=marketing+curve

- When you have a real, usable product, it attracts early adopters. These are people making real products yet who are good at taking and managing risk. They still don't need much help, though they do expect some guarantee that things won't break randomly. This is the bulk of your community.
- When you are in version two or three, you will start to attract the mass market. These are people who expect stability and reliability. They'll ask questions like, "Do you offer support?" Some of these will become contributors. Mostly, however, they are the target paying customers.
- Finally, when you are in later versions, the laggards and skeptics will finally pick up older versions and try them.

It's more complex than this, as you can have multiple overlapping curves. You need to keep the whole market interested, or you lose valuable sections of your community. Each section sells to the next, so you should aim new versions at the evangelists so they can sell them to the pioneers, and so on.

Once you understand the market curve, you see why it's counter-productive to, for instance, write perfect tutorials for the early versions. You won't get the mass market regardless and it will feel patronizing to the pioneers.

Volunteer Burnout

I've emphasized the value of volunteer work as being more accurate, honest, and creative than paid work. There's a strong caveat here. Some of the Social Architecture tools can be dangerous. When you define a compelling mission, you can motivate people close to self-destruction. This was a major problem in the FFII before I took over, made worse by the highly emotional and tribal culture of the organization at that time. Many core members were in a state of deep exhaustion and burnout. It was familiar to me from my own past.

Research into burnout — which you can read on Wikipedia[15] — doesn't seem to match what I've observed in the real world. Data trumps theory, however. Here's what I've seen many times about the specific type of burnout we see in volunteer communities:

* It manifests as a deep disgust with a specific project. We push the project aside, stop answering emails, and might even leave the community. Other people observe that "he's acting strange... depressed, or tired..."

* It is project-related. That is, we burn out on specific projects and not on others. In severe cases, we become dysfunctional for a few months, then begin working again by abandoning the project and starting something else.

* It hits after a period of one to three years, depending on our character and the situation. Very stubborn, driven individuals may take longer to burn out, and when they do, it's worse.

* It is curable. This is the weirdest aspect, which I proved by taking burned-out volunteers and finding money to pay them for what they had been doing for free. They came back happily and carried on successfully.

* It is preventable. Paid staff don't suffer the same kind of burnout. They can definitely get depressed, yet they don't usually just switch off.

Which leads me to conclude that this is about the economics of professional investment. Here's my hypothesis of the mechanisms at play.

Many people invest heavily in their professions, taking great risks especially while young in the hope of reaping rewards later in life. We're able to postpone material rewards for a long time if we think we're on the right track. For example, a young writer or musician will tolerate being poor for many years if he thinks he's on the path to eventual fame and fortune.

---

15   https://en.wikipedia.org/wiki/Occupational_burnout

No matter how subtle, the carrot at the end of the stick is always present in our subconscious. We are essentially economic animals. All of life is economic. We can lie to ourselves really well, yet beneath every act and decision is an economic motive. We invest in projects because we feel they will propel us to success, even if it takes years. We compete with others, trying to find niches where our particular talents can shine.

So it happens that the young mind striving to invest in the right places finds itself in a situation where the weight of lies accumulates and reaches a tipping point. The path suddenly proves itself to be a dead end. The people it was following are manipulative liars. The mission was a fraud. The praise of others is emotional blackmail. The years of investment were a waste, and even a further minute would be wasted.

This type of burnout is like a reckoning. We abandon the project as though it were suddenly toxic, with much the same feeling as if we had eaten something spoiled. Here are some ways to reduce the risk of this happening:

- We cannot work alone on projects. The concentration of all of the responsibility on one person who does not set limits often leads to burnout.
- Projects need a business plan. As long as there is an eventual prospect of economic reward, the mind can survive hard work without material reward for some time.
- Preventative education on burnout can help. When we explain to people what burnout is, they recognize it faster and call for help before it is too late.
- Good tools and processes let us work with less stress and with less dependence on any one person.

The Myth of Individual Intelligence

You will have gathered by now that I'm not a great fan of the brilliance of individuals. Mostly this is because despite being a Mensa member, I've seen myself make such amazingly clever mistakes. Over time I've come to think that the very notion of individual intelligence is a dangerously simplified myth.

In this myth, brilliant individuals think about important problems, and then by hard work and labor, they create solutions and refine those until they are perfect. Sometimes they will have "eureka" moments where they "get" brilliantly simple answers to large problems. The inventor, and the process of invention are rare, precious, and can command a monopoly. History is full of such heroic individuals. We owe them our modern world.

Look more closely, however, and one discovers that this story does not match the facts. History doesn't show lone inventors. It shows lucky people who steal or claim ownership of ideas that are being worked on by many. It shows brilliant people striking lucky, and then spending decades on fruitless and pointless quests. The best-known large-scale inventors like Thomas Edison were good at systematic broad research done by large teams. It's like claiming that Steve Jobs invented every tool made by Apple. It is a nice myth, good for marketing, and utterly untrue.

Recent history, better recorded and less easy to manipulate, shows this well. The Internet is surely one of the most innovative and fast-moving areas of technology, and one of the best documented. It has no inventor. Instead, it has a massive economy of people who have carefully and progressively solved a long series of immediate problems, documented their answers, and made those available to all.

The innovative nature of the Internet comes not from a small, select band of Einsteins. It comes from RFCs anyone can use and improve, made by hundreds and thousands of smart, though not uniquely smart, individuals. It comes from open source software that anyone can use and improve. It comes from sharing, remixing, and scale of community. It comes from the continuous accretion of good solutions, and the disposal of bad ones.

Here thus is an alternative theory of innovation:

1. There is an infinite problem/solution terrain. It is like a landscape of hills and valleys that we are trying to climb. The solutions to interesting problems are at the tops of the hills.

2. This terrain changes over time according to external conditions. Mountains can become flat, and new mountains appear, over time.

3. We can only accurately perceive problems to which we are close. We do not have very long-range vision, only guesses. Our metaphorical landscape is very misty.

4. We can rank the cost/benefit economics of problems using a market for solutions. That is, we can measure how high we are on any given peak.

5. There is an optimal solution to any solvable problem. That is, every slope has a top.

6. We can approach this optimal solution mechanically, by applying the method of taking a step in some approximately good direction, and seeing whether we are now higher or lower than before.

7. Our intelligence can make this process faster, yet does not replace it. Being smarter maybe lets us step faster, or see a little further into the mist, and that's it.

There are a few corollaries to this:

- *Individual creativity matters less than process.* Smarter people may work faster, and they may also work in the wrong direction. It's the collective vision of reality that keeps us honest and relevant.

- *We don't need road maps if we have a good process.* Functionality will emerge and evolve over time as solutions compete for market shares.

- *We don't invent solutions so much as discover them.* All sympathies to the creative soul: it is just an information processing machine that likes to polish its own ego and collect karma.

- *Intelligence is a social effect, though it feels personal.* A person cut off from others eventually stops thinking. We can neither collect problems nor measure solutions without other people.
- *The size and diversity of the community is a key factor.* Larger, more diverse communities collect more relevant problems, solve them more accurately, and do this faster than a small expert group.

So when we trust the solitary experts, they make classic mistakes. They focus on ideas, not problems. They focus on the wrong problems. They make misjudgments about the value of solving problems. And they don't use their own work.

The Collective Intelligence Index, or CII

I'm going to propose a tool to measure the intelligence of a community, in other words, how accurately and efficiently the community is working at any given time. It also measures how enjoyable it will be to participate in the community.

To demonstrate, I'm going to rank a few networks, organizations, websites, and on-line communities. It's not science; it's more like creative abuse of numbers. As everyone knows, 87% of statistics are invented on the spot and 91% of people accept them without question. I've chosen the following victims:

- Wikipedia
- Twitter
- Reddit
- Facebook
- The fashion industry
- The Nigerian movie industry, aka Nollywood
- The military (in some random western nation)
- The Fox News network
- Lawyers, as a profession
- The Hollywood movie industry

I'm not going to make any judgment about the value of any specific community. It's impossible, and would be deceptive. Twitter's implied mission is "collect the most followers," which sounds weak when compared to Wikipedia's "assemble the world's knowledge." Once formed, a smart and agile crowd can just as easily create new missions like "bring down the dictator." Arguably, the value (to society) of an on-line community is not their products, rather it is the community itself. With Wikipedia or ZeroMQ, it's hard to separate the crowd from the content. With Twitter, it's really obvious. The content is transient and mostly worthless, the crowd is not.

Here's the scorecard I came up with:

Criteria	Wk	Tw	Rd	Fb	Fa	Nw	Lw	Hw	FN	Ml
Strong mission	5	3	2	1	2	1	0	0	0	2
Free entry	5	5	5	5	4	3	0	1	2	2
Transparency	5	3	5	1	2	1	0	0	0	0
Free contributors	5	5	5	5	2	3	3	2	1	0
Full remixability	5	5	5	4	4	3	3	1	1	0
Strong protocols	5	5	5	4	4	3	2	3	1	4
Fair authority	5	4	5	3	4	3	1	1	0	1
Non-tribalism	4	5	5	5	3	3	0	2	0	0
Self-organization	5	5	5	5	4	4	2	2	0	0
Tolerance	5	5	5	5	4	3	2	3	0	0
Measurable success	5	5	5	5	5	5	4	5	5	2
High scoring	3	5	5	5	4	3	3	2	1	1
Decentralization	5	5	5	5	5	1	1	1	0	1
Free workspaces	5	5	5	5	3	2	0	0	0	0
Smooth learning	4	5	5	5	3	3	0	1	0	0
Regular structure	5	5	5	4	3	2	3	3	1	5
Positivity	5	5	5	5	5	3	0	2	0	0
Sense of humor	5	5	5	5	2	3	0	1	1	0
Minimalism	5	5	4	4	3	4	1	1	3	0
Sane funding	5	4	3	3	5	3	3	3	2	2
Final score	96	94	94	84	71	56	28	34	18	20

Once we can measure the CII of a community or organization, we can increase it by looking at the tools that score low. In theory, this should make the organization smarter, and its participants happier. Of course it's quite likely that a military organization can only work with a low CII. A smart army would quite likely all go home and switch to Reddit.

How to Capture an Open Source Project

Ars Technica has an interesting article[16] on how Google is closing off Android piece by piece. It is a classic game of "capture the flag", played against an open source community. I'm going to explain how this capture works, and how to prevent it.

Why Capture the Flag?

As Ars Technica says, "It's easy to give something away when you're in last place with zero marketshare, precisely where Android started. When you're in first place though, it's a little harder to be so open and welcoming."

Android is, to be fair, largely Google's investment. You could argue that they are entirely justified to turn it from an open system into a closed one, and you'd be right. However, it is like arguing that a central bank is entirely justified in issuing too much currency and creating devaluation. Sure, there is a justification. However there is also a cost, paid by other people. The question is not, is this act justified, but is the price paid by wider society acceptable, and if not, how do we prevent it?

Android is, like any "open source" system sold to the market on that basis, common property. When someone privatizes it, they are increasing their profits, like a money-printing central bank, at the expense of everyone else. By forking Android applications like search,

---

16   http://arstechnica.com/gadgets/2013/10/googles-iron-grip-on-android-controlling-open-source-by-any-means-necessary/

calendar, music, and making their own better versions, Google is competing with other firms using Android on their devices.

The question of capture, how it happens, and how to prevent it, is especially important if you are *not* Google, i.e. if you are the user of, or a contributor to, an open source project. Android contains many patches from other firms, like LG, Samsung, and so on. As Google turns the operating system into its own private garden, those patches start to be used *against* the very people who made them.

I believe Google is making a huge mistake in moving the goalposts like this, simply because it will encourage competition against Android. However, that's not my point. I'm just interested in applying any lessons I can learn to my own work, and my own projects.

Two things stand out:

• Out of pure self-interest, I will not contribute to an open source project that does not guarantee me, as contributor, that my patches and changes will never be turned into private code, and used against me.

• Out of a sense of ethics, I will never create an open source project that does not provide these guarantees to anyone contributing to it.

The Use Case

Let me be very explicit about the use case. It is the Android case: one firm starting an open source project as loss leader, to break an existing market, and asking for help from others to do so. It is a classic strategy and can be very successful. However this is most definitely not the same as a student's research project, a "let's open source our legacy payroll system" dump, or a "five of us got together in a garage and decided to make a new framework" case.

These overlap, and I think the lessons here do apply more widely (and I certainly apply them *systematically*) yet again, my use-case is the "open source as market breaker" one.

The important thing about an open source market breaker is that it depends on a community to pitch in. Any market follows a power curve where a few players dominate the market, and a majority of players are frustrated. It's by promising this frustrated crowd a way out, that you can convince them to invest in something new and open and potentially game-changing.

Most open source is a failure (seriously, go read some random Git-Hub projects and see how many are relevant), and even most successes are modest successes that barely matter. As long as there's no serious shift in power, the project can remain a potential market breaker for a long time. It can look very stable and happy. Well, it's easy to be friendly when there's no money on the table.

If and when the project succeeds, the game changes, and the clever guys who launched the market breaker seek to pluck the fruit, and keep it for themselves. And only now do things get interesting.

A Level Playing Field is Not "Restrictive"

There are several ways to capture an open source project, including trademarks and patents. I'm going to look only at copyrights, because this is the most common case. The key agreements that govern the copyright status of an open source project are (a) the license and (b) the contribution policy.

It's a common misconception that "open source" means the code cannot be captured. That is simply wrong. Broadly, there are three types of agreement for copyright:

1. A "locked down" license that does not allow remixing, in other words, classic copyright plus some restrictive license.
2. A "free to take" license that allows one-way remixing, such as Apache/BSD/MIT.
3. A "share-alike" license that enforces two-way remixing, such as GPL, LGPL, and cc-by-sa.

Imagine a DJ who releases a popular beat under the "free to take" model. A major record label takes his beat and makes a remix, and releases it. It becomes a massive hit. Now that new version is locked down. The DJ cannot remix that new work, and may find himself unable even to play the remix. Sure, he can take his old version and improve it, yet it's the commercial version that will get the money.

I trust you see what I am getting at here. Even the best individual talent cannot compete equally with a large firm with marketing and money. The only way I know to guarantee a level playing field in a war of control over culture is a *bilateral guarantee of remixing*. Bilateral means it goes two ways.

When people call that guarantee "restrictive", I sigh. It's like calling the lock in my car "restrictive" because it stops others from making my car theirs. To call protection from thieves "restrictive" is... well, a failure to think things through, at least. Making rules apply both ways is not restrictive, OK!?

How Does the Capture Work?

Let's clearly restate the goal again, with this exercise. It is to prevent the capture of an open source project by someone with lots of money and power, who is determined to harvest the fruits of the project for their own benefit, at the cost of the community who helped make, or who made the project. I don't care how "justified" such a capture might be, it's what I'm explaining how to prevent.

The license and contribution policy are two halves of one puzzle.

Who owns the copyrights? Are they "centralized" by the project founders, or are they shared by all contributors? It's a vital question. If they are centralized then it is a trivial exercise to buy the copyrights, fork the project, change the license unilaterally, and move off in a closed direction. However, if the copyrights are shared, i.e. many people own the work, together, you need all of their agreement (not a majority, but 100% consensus) to change the license. And that is logistically impossible.

As an aside, if you knew how many people had offered me money for a commercial license for ZeroMQ, you would be astonished (it is a lot). The notion is simple: I sell them a non-LGPL license, they pay me good money, and they make their own versions of ZeroMQ. If I'd not made this impossible, on purpose, a long time ago, I'd be very wealthy. As it is, I have to settle with poor but happy in the knowledge that ZeroMQ will survive me.

Let's examine again the problem with offering commercial licenses to a collaborative work on the side. Imagine a club that hosts DJs, who mix their beats. But the club keeps the copyrights, and sells them to a record label, which makes its own remixed album *that the original DJs cannot play for free*. So yes, I consider dual GPL/commercial licensing to be a corrupt practice.

No-one will pay for a commercial license for a "free to take" project, since they can just take the code and use it. To some extent I think that is already corrupt, since it breaks the level playing field. A large firm can obviously benefit more from such a license than small teams. Again, imagine your independent DJs against a record label with their marketing and media connections and concert venues.

Now we come to step two of the capture: hire the developers.

"But the code is still free!", people say. Sure. Back to the record label vs. the DJs. Let's say the label hires just one DJ, the key man, and uses him to push the new commercial mix album. Where is the public going to go?

You don't need to hire all the contributors to a community in order to own it. In any random project there will be at most 2-3 top contributors and a large mass of minor ones. Hire the top two, and you can take the project anywhere you like. If the results are remixable, that journey will be entirely fair to those who contributed before. And if not remixable, all other contributors will find their own investments used against them.

Preventing Capture

There is only one model I know that prevents capture of an open source software project, and that is:

1. A GPL-family license (or MPLv2, which works the same).
2. Distributed copyrights.

This is how I construct the open source projects I start, and it's the requirement for any community I join. Your right to make money does not include the right to use my work in a competing product, unless that's reciprocal.

Legal primer: Trademarks

Trademarks. What are they, do you need them, and how much do they cost? These are questions that often crop up when we build open source projects. Trademarks can be key to protecting a project from bad actors. Yet there is little advice on line. So here is my guide to using trademarks in open source. This is practical advice, IANAL, and certainly not your lawyer.

A Background to Trademarks

Definitions first. A trademark is a name, phrase, logo, or even a specific color (the "mark") that you're using for business ("trade"). The simple fact of using a mark for some period of time establishes the trademark. However as with all property, the devil lies in enforcement. The question is, always, if you go before a judge with a complaint, what standards of evidence will the judge expect and demand?

No matter the case, criminal or civil, it always comes down to convincing one or more humans. If you ever go to court, keep this in mind. The facts of a case, as each party knows them, are irrelevant. How those facts are documented and presented is all that matters.

Let's back up a little and ask why courts even care about protecting businesses' trademarks. First, it's to protect consumers from misleading sales tactics. Just selling junk isn't an offense as such, except when there are legal minimum standards for health and safety. However selling junk that claims to be a more expensive, well-known brand is an offense. So secondly, trademarks let businesses distinguish themselves and stop unfair competition.

So the judge in a trademark violation case will ask, "Was the intent to deceive the consumer? Would a reasonable consumer be deceived?" And then the judge will ask, "Who owned the trademark, and can they prove it?" Even though the simple act using a mark creates it (under so-called Common Law), that can be hard to establish.

For instance, business A creates a chain of restaurants. Business B opens a competing chain using the same colors and similar name. B is clearly hijacking A's investment in branding, stealing goodwill. Yet when A takes B to court, B produces a document showing their restaurant plans, a full year before A started. How does the judge know who is the liar?

In clear cut cases, you can convince a judge that a copycat is deceiving consumers and stealing your goodwill. Yet the risk of losing such a case is high. It's also costly for courts to deal with such cases. Judges may simply refuse to hear them.

Hence most countries provide a way to register your marks, for a fee. Registration gives you a dated document that establishes your claim to the mark. The trademark office does the job of searching for prior marks in the same area. Before it grants you the registration, it publishes your claim and gives others a chance to dispute it. So after a search, and if there are no disputes, a judge will take the trademark registration as solid evidence.

It is not that simple. A competitor can still claim that their Common Law mark outweighs your registered trademark. They can argue that the registration does not represent real goodwill. This is often understood as, "if you don't enforce your mark, you will lose it," which is inaccurate. As trademark holder you're not expected to police the world. However you are expected to be truthful in court when the judge asks you, "are you using your mark, and suffering real damage due to the unfair competition?"

Finally, courts consider trademarks to apply per segment of the market. So you can have XYZ Car Co, and XYZ Clothing Co, with no confusion to the market. When you register a mark you'll need to explain what "classes" you're using it in. You'll probably want international class 9, which is anything that beeps.

Where and How to Register

If you are large enough to need to register in multiple countries then you are large enough to have trademark lawyers. For the rest of us, it's a bit like buying a domain name. Sure, there are hundreds of domain extensions. Yet we still want a dot-com for our main business.

So it is with trademarks. If you decide to register a mark, do it in the US (via the USPTO) first. That's cheap, and simple. Then over time you can register in the EU (via the OHIM), if you find your project is worth it.

The cost for a US registration is around USD 1500, depending on what lawyer you use. You can find trademark attorneys on line. They'll ask you for details of the mark, proof that it's being used, name and address of the registrant, and credit card details. The process takes about six months. After nine years (and before ten years have passed) you can renew the mark.

Getting a US registration will speed up registration in other countries, if you decide to apply for that later. The risk, and it's a small one, is that a troll will register your trademark in some other country, effectively excluding you from doing business under that name, there.

Before you register, however, ask yourself "what is the chance someone would rip off my name and logo?" If it's low, don't bother. If it's high, then ask "what is the chance a cheat would take this to court?" If that is still low, then don't bother either.

Instead of registering a mark you can raise its visibility. This means being explicit on your website and other materials. "X, Y, and Z are trademarks of MyCorp." This scares off potential cheats, improves

your case, if you do try to defend the mark in court, and makes it easier to get registration if and when you need it.

How to Enforce your Trademark

Registered or not, you enforce your mark by telling the other party,
in writing, "stop now, or else." If they do not stop, you repeat the
warning, with initial claims of damages. If they do not stop, you add
on more damages and when you have a solid file, you take it to court.

The vast majority of people will back-off at once. The trouble is
when you face someone who's well aware of trademark law, has cheap
legal resources, and enjoys time in court.

If you are facing such a firm, and you did not register your mark,
you should probably fold your hand, and change your name. The
risks are high that you would lose, and have high legal fees and pos-
sibly damages to pay. Judges don't always get it right.

If you did register your mark, then you should push ahead and
claim damages. You will win, if you stick to the basic rules (you're still
using the mark, the damages are real.) Do I need to say, any court case
will have to happen in the country of registration? Judges in Belgium
won't accept paper from the USPTO.

Trademarks For Open Source Projects

The common misconception about open source is that because the
code is free, it does represents no property nor value. The opposite is
true: successful projects represent considerable value, owned by many.
How does a trademark represent and protect that value?

It comes down to authenticity and reputation. If you download a
package calling itself "XYZ v2.0", then you may have expectations. It
is compatible; it works; it has no trojans or advertising; it is from the
same people as "XYZ v1.0".

If a successful project does not register its name, then anyone can
fork it, repackage it, and use the same name. Imagine competing, incompatible versions of "Linux."

When a person or a business registers the name as a trademark, those incompatible forks may still exist. However they may not use the mark. If they try to do that, it's damages time.

I've had this happen at least once in my own projects, and the trademark was the tool I used to stop the incompatible forks and punish the perpetrators. Trademark law is clear enough that saying "trademark violation" will stop 99% of cheats dead still. Producing a registration filing number stops 99% of the remainder.

In a serious project like ZeroMQ you'll end up with three or four marks you want to register, over a period of five to ten years. Register only when it's worth it. That is, to protect real trademarks that you would be willing to defend in court. Consider that in the worst case you might have to spend ten or twenty times the cost of registration, to defend your mark. You might get that back, or you might now.

I hope this small brief has helped you understand trademarks, and how to use them (or not) in your open source projects. And, if someone claims you're infringing on their trademark, how to defend yourself. (Hint: ask them for a registration number.)

Chapter 3. The ZeroMQ Community

People sometimes ask me what's so special about ZeroMQ. My standard answer is that ZeroMQ is arguably the best answer we have to the vexing question of "How do we make the distributed software that the 21st century demands?" But more than that, ZeroMQ is special because of its community. This is ultimately what separates the wolves from the sheep.

There are three main open source patterns. The first is the large firm dumping code to break the market for others. This is the Apache Foundation model. The second is tiny teams or small firms building their dream. This is the most common open source model, which can be very successful commercially. The last is aggressive and diverse communities that swarm over a problem landscape. This is the Linux model, and the one to which we aspire with ZeroMQ.

It's hard to overemphasize the power and persistence of a working open source community. There really does not seem to be a better way of making software for the long term. Not only does the community choose the best problems to solve, it solves them minimally, carefully, and it then looks after these answers for years, decades, until they're no longer relevant, and then it quietly puts them away.

To really benefit from ZeroMQ, you need to understand the community. At some point down the road you'll want to submit a patch, an issue, or an add-on. You might want to ask someone for help. You will probably want to bet a part of your business on ZeroMQ, and when I tell you that the community is much, much more important than the company that backs the product, even though I'm CEO of that company, this should be significant.

In this section I'm going to look at our community from several angles and conclude by explaining in detail our contract for collaboration, which we call "C4"[17]. You should find the discussion useful for your own work. We've also adapted the ZeroMQ C4 process for closed source projects with good success.

Architecture of the ZeroMQ Community

You know that ZeroMQ is an LGPL-licensed project (author's note: we are moving towards the Mozilla Public License v2, which has the same effect yet is simpler). In fact it's a collection of projects, built around the core library, libzmq. I'll visualize these projects as an expanding galaxy:

- At the core, libzmq is the ZeroMQ core library. It's written in C++, with a low-level C API. The code is nasty, mainly because it's highly optimized but also because it's written in C++, a language that lends itself to subtle and deep nastiness. Martin Sustrik wrote the bulk of the original code. Today it has dozens of people who maintain different parts of it.

- Around libzmq, there are about 50 *bindings*. These are individual projects that create higher-level APIs for ZeroMQ, or at least map the low-level API into other languages. The bindings vary in quality from experimental to utterly awesome. Probably the most impressive binding is PyZMQ[18], which was one of the first community projects on top of ZeroMQ. If you are a binding author, you should really study PyZMQ and aspire to making your code and community as great.

- A lot of languages have multiple bindings (Erlang, Ruby, C#, at least) written by different people over time, or taking varying approaches. We don't regulate these in any way. There are no "official" bindings. You vote by using one or the other, contributing to it, or ignoring it.

- There are a series of reimplementations of libzmq, starting with JeroMQ, a full Java translation of the library, which is now the

---

17   http://rfc.zeromq.org/spec:42

18   https://github.com/zeromq/pyzmq

basis for NetMQ, a C# stack. These native stacks offer similar or identical APIs, and speak the same protocol (ZMTP) as libzmq.

- On top of the bindings are thousands of projects that use ZeroMQ or build on it. Some of these like Zyre and Malamute are part of the "official" community, most are not.

Libzmq, most of the bindings, and some of the outer projects sit in the ZeroMQ community "organization"[19] on GitHub. This organization is "run" by a group consisting of the most senior binding authors. There's very little to run as it's almost all self-managing and there's zero conflict these days.

iMatix, my firm, plays a specific role in the community. We own the trademarks and enforce them discretely in order to make sure that if you download a package calling itself "ZeroMQ", you can trust what you are getting. People have on rare occasion tried to hijack the name, maybe believing that "free software" means there is no property at stake and no one willing to defend it. One thing you'll understand from this article is how seriously we take the process behind our software (and I mean "us" as a community, not a company). iMatix backs the community by enforcing that process on anything calling itself "ZeroMQ" or "ZeroMQ". We also put money and time into the software and packaging for reasons I'll explain later.

It is not a charity exercise. ZeroMQ is a for-profit project, and a very profitable one. The profits are widely distributed among all those who invest in it. It's really that simple: take the time to become an expert in ZeroMQ, or build something useful on top of ZeroMQ, and you'll find your value as an individual, or team, or company increasing. iMatix enjoys the same benefits as everyone else in the community. It's win-win to everyone except our competitors, who find themselves facing a threat they can't beat and can't really escape. ZeroMQ dominates the future world of massively distributed software.

---

19   https://github.com/organizations/zeromq

My firm doesn't just have the community's back—we also built the community. This was deliberate work; in the original ZeroMQ white paper from 2007, there were two projects. One was technical, how to make a better messaging system. The second was how to build a community that could take the software to dominant success. Software dies, but community survives.

How to Make Really Large Architectures

There are, it has been said (at least by people reading this sentence out loud), two ways to make really large-scale software. Option One is to throw massive amounts of money and problems at empires of smart people, and hope that what emerges is not yet another career killer. If you're very lucky and are building on lots of experience, have kept your teams solid, and are not aiming for technical brilliance, and are furthermore incredibly lucky, it works.

But gambling with hundreds of millions of others' money isn't for everyone. For the rest of us who want to build large-scale software, there's Option Two, which is open source, and more specifically, *free software*. If you're asking how the choice of software license is relevant to the scale of the software you build, that's the right question.

The brilliant and visionary Eben Moglen once said, roughly, that a free software license is the contract on which a community builds. When I heard this, about ten years ago, the idea came to me— *Can we deliberately grow free software communities?*

Ten years later, the answer is "yes", and there is almost a science to it. I say "almost" because we don't yet have enough evidence of people doing this deliberately with a documented, reproducible process. It is what I'm trying to do with Social Architecture[20]. ZeroMQ came after Wikidot, after the Digital Standards Organization[21] (Digistan) and after the Foundation for a Free Information Infrastruc-

---

20   http://cultureandempire.com/cande.html#/4/6

21   http://www.digistan.org

ture[22] (aka the FFII, an NGO that fights against software patents). This all came after a lot of less successful community projects like Xitami and Libero. My main takeaway from a long career of projects of every conceivable format is: if you want to build truly large-scale and long-lasting software, aim to build a free software community.

Psychology of Software Architecture

Dirkjan Ochtman pointed me to Wikipedia's definition of Software Architecture[23] as "the set of structures needed to reason about the system, which comprise software elements, relations among them, and properties of both". For me this vapid and circular jargon is a good example of how miserably little we understand what actually makes a successful large scale software architecture.

Architecture is the art and science of making large artificial structures for human use. If there is one thing I've learned and applied successfully in 30 years of making larger and larger software systems, it is this: *software is about people*. Large structures in themselves are meaningless. It's how they function for *human use* that matters. And in software, human use starts with the programmers who make the software itself.

The core problems in software architecture are driven by human psychology, not technology. There are many ways our psychology affects our work. I could point to the way teams seem to get stupider as they get larger or when they have to work across larger distances. Does that mean the smaller the team, the more effective? How then does a large global community like ZeroMQ manage to work successfully?

The ZeroMQ community wasn't accidental. It was a deliberate design, my contribution to the early days when the code came out of a cellar in Bratislava. The design was based on my pet science of "Social Architecture", which Wikipedia defines[24] as "the conscious design of

22 http://www.ffii.org
23 http://en.wikipedia.org/wiki/Software_architecture
24 http://en.wikipedia.org/wiki/Social_architecture

an environment that encourages a desired range of social behaviors leading towards some goal or set of goals." I define this as more specifically as "the process, and the product, of planning, designing, and growing an online community."

One of the tenets of Social Architecture is that *how we organize* is more significant than *who we are*. The same group, organized differently, can produce wholly different results. We are like peers in a ZeroMQ network, and our communication patterns have a dramatic impact on our performance. Ordinary people, well connected, can far outperform a team of experts using poor patterns. If you're the architect of a larger ZeroMQ application, you're going to have to help others find the right patterns for working together. Do this right, and your project can succeed. Do it wrong, and your project will fail.

The two most important psychological elements are that we're really bad at understanding complexity and that we are so good at working together to divide and conquer large problems. We're highly social apes, and kind of smart, but only in the right kind of crowd.

So here is my short list of the Psychological Elements of Software Architecture:

- **Stupidity**: our mental bandwidth is limited, so we're all stupid at some point. The architecture has to be simple to understand. This is the number one rule: simplicity beats functionality, every single time. If you can't understand an architecture on a cold gray Monday morning before coffee, it is too complex.

- **Selfishness**: we act only out of self-interest, so the architecture must create space and opportunity for selfish acts that benefit the whole. Selfishness is often indirect and subtle. For example, I'll spend hours helping someone else understand something because that could be worth days to me later.

- **Laziness**: we make lots of assumptions, many of which are wrong. We are happiest when we can spend the least effort to get a result or to test an assumption quickly, so the architecture has to make this possible. Specifically, that means it must be simple.

- **Jealousy**: we're jealous of others, which means we'll overcome our stupidity and laziness to prove others wrong and beat them in competition. The architecture thus has to create space for public competition based on fair rules that anyone can understand.

- **Fear**: we're unwilling to take risks, especially if it makes us look stupid. Fear of failure is a major reason people conform and follow the group in mass stupidity. The architecture should make silent experimentation easy and cheap, giving people opportunity for success without punishing failure.

- **Reciprocity**: we'll pay extra in terms of hard work, even money, to punish cheats and enforce fair rules. The architecture should be heavily rule-based, telling people how to work together, but not what to work on.

- **Conformity**: we're happiest to conform, out of fear and laziness, which means if the patterns are good, clearly explained and documented, and fairly enforced, we'll naturally choose the right path every time.

- **Pride**: we're intensely aware of our social status, and we'll work hard to avoid looking stupid or incompetent in public. The architecture has to make sure every piece we make has our name on it, so we'll have sleepless nights stressing about what others will say about our work.

- **Greed**: we're ultimately economic animals (see selfishness), so the architecture has to give us economic incentive to invest in making it happen. Maybe it's polishing our reputation as experts, maybe it's literally making money from some skill or component. It doesn't matter what it is, but there must be economic incentive. Think of architecture as a market place, not an engineering design.

These strategies work on a large scale but also on a small scale, within an organization or team.

The Importance of Contracts

Let me discuss a contentious but important area, which is what license to choose. I'll say "BSD" to cover MIT, Xɪɪ, BSD, Apache, and similar licenses, and "GPL" to cover GPLv3, LGPLv3, and AGPLv3. The significant difference is the obligation to share back any forked versions, which prevents any entity from capturing the software, and thus keeps it "free".

A software license isn't technically a contract since you don't sign anything. But broadly, calling it a contract is useful since it takes the obligations of each party, and makes them legally enforceable in court, under copyright law.

You might ask, why do we need contracts at all to make open source? Surely it's all about decency, goodwill, people working together for selfless motives. Surely the principle of "less is more" applies here of all places? Don't more rules mean less freedom? Do we really need lawyers to tell us how to work together? It seems cynical and even counter-productive to force a restrictive set of rules on the happy communes of free and open source software.

But the truth about human nature is not that pretty. We're not really angels, nor devils, just self-interested winners descended from a billion-year unbroken line of winners. In business, marriage, and collective works, sooner or later, we either stop caring, or we fight and we argue.

Put this another way: a collective work has two extreme outcomes. Either it's a failure, irrelevant, and worthless, in which case every sane person walks away, without a fight. Or, it's a success, relevant, and valuable, in which case we start jockeying for power, control, and often, money.

What a well-written contract does is to protect those valuable relationships from conflict. A marriage where the terms of divorce are clearly agreed up-front is much less likely to end in divorce. A business deal where both parties agree how to resolve various classic conflicts—such as one party stealing the others' clients or staff—is much less likely to end in conflict.

Similarly, a software project that has a well-written contract that defines the terms of breakup clearly is much less likely to end in breakup. The alternative seems to be to immerse the project into a larger organization that can assert pressure on teams to work together (or lose the backing and branding of the organization). This is for example how the Apache Foundation works. In my experience organization building has its own costs, and ends up favoring wealthier participants (who can afford those sometimes huge costs).

In an open source or free software project, breakup usually takes the form of a fork, where the community splits into two or more groups, each with different visions of the future. During the honeymoon period of a project, which can last years, there's no question of a breakup. It is as a project begins to be worth money, or as the main authors start to burn out, that the goodwill and generosity tends to dry up.

So when discussing software licenses, for the code you write or the code you use, a little cynicism helps. Ask yourself, not "which license will attract more contributors?" because the answer to that lies in the mission statement and contribution process. Ask yourself, "if this project had a big fight, and split three ways, which license would save us?" Or, "if the whole team was bought by a hostile firm that wanted to turn this code into a proprietary product, which license would save us?"

Long-term survival means enduring the bad times, as well as enjoying the good ones.

When BSD projects fork, they cannot easily merge again. Indeed, one-way forking of BSD projects is quite systematic: every time BSD code ends up in a commercial project, this is what's happened. When GPL projects fork, however, re-merging is trivial.

The GPL's story is relevant here. Though communities of programmers sharing their code openly were already significant by the 1980's, they tended to use minimal licenses that worked as long as no real money got involved. There was an important language stack called Emacs, originally built in Lisp by Richard Stallman. Another programmer, James Gosling (who later gave us Java), rewrote Emacs in C with the help of many contributors, on the assumption that it would be open. Stallman got that code and used it as the basis for his own C version. Gosling then sold the code to a firm which turned around and blocked anyone distributing a competing product. Stallman found this sale of the common work hugely unethical, and began developing a reusable license that would protect communities from this.

What eventually emerged was the GNU General Public License, which used traditional copyright to force remixability. It was a neat hack that spread to other domains, for instance the Creative Commons for photography and music. In 2007, we saw version 3 of the license, which was a response to belated attacks from Microsoft and others on the concept. It has become a long and complex document but corporate copyright lawyers have become familiar with it and in my experience, few companies mind using GPL software and libraries, so long as the boundaries are clearly defined.

Thus, a good contract—and I consider the modern GPL to be the best for software—lets programmers work together without upfront agreements, organizations, or assumptions of decency and goodwill. It makes it cheaper to collaborate, and turns conflict into healthy competition. GPL doesn't just define what happens with a fork, it actively encourages forks as a tool for experimentation and learning. Whereas a fork can kill a project with a "more liberal" license, GPL projects thrive on forks since successful experiments can, by contract, be remixed back into the mainstream.

Yes, there are many thriving BSD projects and many dead GPL ones. It's always wrong to generalize. A project will thrive or die for many reasons. However, in a competitive sport, one needs every advantage.

The other important part of the BSD vs. GPL story is what I call "leakage", which is the effect of pouring water into a pot with a small but real hole in the bottom.

Eat Me

Here is a story. It happened to the eldest brother-in-law of the cousin of a friend of mine's colleague at work. His name was, and still is, Patrick.

Patrick was a computer scientist with a PhD in advanced network topologies. He spent two years and his savings building a new product, and choose the BSD license because he believed that would get him more adoption. He worked in his attic, at great personal cost, and proudly published his work. People applauded, for it was truly fantastic, and his mailing lists were soon abuzz with activity and patches and happy chatter. Many companies told him how they were saving millions using his work. Some of them even paid him for consultancy and training. He was invited to speak at conferences and started collecting badges with his name on them. He started a small business, hired a friend to work with him, and dreamed of making it big.

Then one day, someone pointed him to a new project, GPL licensed, which had forked his work and was improving on it. He was irritated and upset, and asked how people—fellow open sourcers, no less!—would so shamelessly steal his code. There were long arguments on the list about whether it was even legal to relicense their BSD code as GPL code. Turned out, it was. He tried to ignore the new project, but then he soon realized that new patches coming from that project *couldn't even be merged back* into his work!

Worse, the GPL project got popular and some of his core contributors made first small, and then larger patches to it. Again, he couldn't use those changes, and he felt abandoned. Patrick went into a depression, his girlfriend left him for an international currency dealer called, weirdly, Patrice, and he stopped all work on the project. He felt betrayed, and utterly miserable. He fired his friend, who took it rather badly and told everyone that Patrick was a closet banjo player. Finally, Patrick took a job as a project manager for a cloud company, and by the age of forty, he had stopped programming even for fun.

Poor Patrick. I almost felt sorry for him. Then I asked him, "Why didn't you choose the GPL?" "Because it's a restrictive viral license", he replied. I told him, "You may have a PhD, and you may be the eldest brother-in-law of the cousin of a friend of my colleague, but you are an idiot and Monique was smart to leave you. You published your work inviting people to please steal your code as long as they kept this 'please steal my code' statement in the resulting work", and when people did exactly that, you got upset. Worse, you were a hypocrite because when they did it in secret, you were happy, but when they did it openly, you felt betrayed."

Seeing your hard work captured by a smarter team and then used against you is enormously painful, so why even make that possible? Every proprietary project that uses BSD code is capturing it. A public GPL fork is perhaps more humiliating, but it's fully self-inflicted.

BSD is like food. It literally (and I mean that metaphorically) whispers "eat me" in the little voice one imagines a cube of cheese might use when it's sitting next to an empty bottle of the best beer in the world, which is of course Orval, brewed by an ancient and almost extinct order of silent Belgian monks called *Les Gars Labas Qui Fabrique l'Orval*. The BSD license, like its near clone MIT/X11, was designed specifically by a university (Berkeley) with no profit motive to leak work and effort. It is a way to push subsidized technology at below its cost price, a dumping of under-priced code in the hope that it will break the market for others. BSD is an *excellent* strategic tool, but only if you're a large well-funded institution that can afford to use Option One. The Apache license is BSD in a suit.

For us small businesses who aim our investments like precious bullets, leaking work and effort is unacceptable. Breaking the market is great, but we cannot afford to subsidize our competitors. The BSD networking stack ended up putting Windows on the Internet. We cannot afford battles with those we should naturally be allies with. We cannot afford to make fundamental business errors because in the end, that means we have to fire people.

It comes down to behavioral economics and game theory. *The license we choose modifies the economics of those who use our work.* In the software industry, there are friends, foes, and food. BSD makes most people see us as lunch. Closed source makes most people see us as enemies (do you *like* paying people for software?) GPL, however, makes most people, with the exception of the Patricks of the world, our allies. Any fork of ZeroMQ is license compatible with ZeroMQ, to the point where we *encourage* forks as a valuable tool for experimentation. Yes, it can be weird to see someone try to run off with the ball but here's the secret, *I can get it back any time I want.*

The Process

If you've accepted my thesis up to now, great! Now, I'll explain the rough process by which we actually build an open source community. This was how we built or grew or gently steered the ZeroMQ community into existence.

Your goal as leader of a community is to motivate people to get out there and explore; to ensure they can do so safely and without disturbing others; to reward them when they make successful discoveries; and to ensure they share their knowledge with everyone else (and not because we ask them, not because they feel generous, but because it's The Law).

It is an iterative process. You make a small product, at your own cost, but in public view. You then build a small community around that product. If you have a small but real hit, the community then helps design and build the next version, and grows larger. And then that community builds the next version, and so on. It's evident that you remain part of the community, maybe even a majority contributor, but the more control you try to assert over the material results, the less people will want to participate. Plan your own retirement well before someone decides you are their next problem.

Crazy, Beautiful, and Easy

You need a goal that's crazy and simple enough to get people out of bed in the morning. Your community has to attract the very best people and that demands something special. With ZeroMQ, we said we were going to make "the Fastest. Messaging. Ever.", which qualifies as a good motivator. If we'd said, we're going to make "a smart transport layer that'll connect your moving pieces cheaply and flexibly across your enterprise", we'd have failed.

Then your work must be beautiful, immediately useful, and attractive. Your contributors are users who want to explore just a little beyond where they are now. Make it simple, elegant, and brutally clean. The experience when people run or use your work should be an emotional one. They should *feel* something, and if you accurately solved even just one big problem that until then they didn't quite realize they faced, you'll have a small part of their soul.

It must be easy to understand, use, and join. Too many projects have barriers to access: put yourself in the other person's mind and see all the reasons they come to your site, thinking "Um, interesting project, but..." and then leave. You want them to stay and try it, just once. Use GitHub and put the issue tracker right there.

If you do these things well, your community will be smart but more importantly, it will be intellectually and geographically diverse. This is really important. A group of like-minded experts cannot explore the problem landscape well. They tend to make big mistakes. Diversity beats education any time.

Stranger, Meet Stranger

How much up-front agreement do two people need to work together on something? In most organizations, a lot. But you can bring this cost down to near-zero, and then people can collaborate without having ever met, done a phone conference, meeting, or business trip to discuss Roles and Responsibilities over way too many bottles of cheap Korean rice wine.

You need well-written rules that are designed by cynical people like me to force strangers into mutually beneficial collaboration instead of conflict. The GPL is a good start. GitHub and its fork/merge strategy is a good follow-up. And then you want something like our C4 rule-book[25] to control how work actually happens.

C4 (which I now use for every new open source project) has detailed and tested answers to a lot of common mistakes people make, such as the sin of working offline in a corner with others "because it's faster". Transparency is essential to get trust, which is essential to get scale. By forcing every single change through a single transparent pro-cess, you build real trust in the results.

Another cardinal sin that many open source developers make is to place themselves above others. "I founded this project thus my intel-lect is superior to that of others". It's not just immodest and rude, and usually inaccurate, it's also poor business. The rules must apply equally to everyone, without distinction. You are part of the com-munity. Your job, as founder of a project, is not to impose your vision of the product over others, but to make sure the rules are good, hon-est, and *enforced.*

Infinite Property

One of the saddest myths of the knowledge business is that ideas are a sensible form of property. It's medieval nonsense that should have been junked along with slavery, but sadly it's still making too many powerful people too much money.

Ideas are cheap. What does work sensibly as property is the hard work we do in building a market. "You eat what you kill" is the right model for encouraging people to work hard. Whether it's moral au-thority over a project, money from consulting, or the sale of a trade-

---

25   http://rfc.zeromq.org/spec:42

mark to some large, rich firm: if you make it, you own it. But what you really own is "footfall", participants in your project, which ultimately defines your power.

To do this requires infinite free space. Thankfully, GitHub solved this problem for us, for which I will die a grateful person (there are many reasons to be grateful in life, which I won't list here because we only have a hundred or so pages left, but this is one of them).

You cannot scale a single project with many owners like you can scale a collection of many small projects, each with fewer owners. When we embrace forks, a person can become an "owner" with a single click. Now they just have to convince others to join by demonstrating their unique value.

So in ZeroMQ, we aimed to make it easy to write bindings on top of the core library, and we stopped trying to make those bindings ourselves. This created space for others to make those, become their owners, and get that credit.

Care and Feeding

I wish a community could be 100% self-steering, and perhaps one day this will work, but today it's not the case. We're very close with ZeroMQ, but from my experience a community needs four types of care and feeding:

- First, simply because most people are too nice, we need some kind of symbolic leadership or owners who provide ultimate authority in case of conflict. Usually it's the founders of the community. I've seen it work with self-elected groups of "elders", but old men like to talk a lot. I've seen communities split over the question "who is in charge?", and setting up legal entities with boards and such seems to make arguments over control worse, not better. Maybe because there seems to be more to fight over. One of the real benefits of free software is that it's always remixable, so instead of fighting over a pie, one simply forks the pie.

- Second, communities need living rules, and thus they need a lawyer able to formulate and write these down. Rules are critical; when done right, they remove friction. When done wrong, or neglected, we see real friction and argument that can drive away the nice majority, leaving the argumentative core in charge of the burning house. One thing I've tried to do with the ZeroMQ and previous communities is create reusable rules, which perhaps means we don't need lawyers as much.

- Thirdly, communities need some kind of financial backing. This is the jagged rock that breaks most ships. If you starve a community, it becomes more creative but the core contributors burn out. If you pour too much money into it, you attract the professionals, who never say "no", and the community loses its diversity and creativity. If you create a fund for people to share, they will fight (bitterly) over it. With ZeroMQ, we (iMatix) spend our time and money on marketing and packaging (like this book), and the basic care, like bug fixes, releases, and websites.

- Lastly, sales and commercial mediation are important. There is a natural market between expert contributors and customers, but both are somewhat incompetent at talking to each other. Customers assume that support is free or very cheap because the software is free. Contributors are shy at asking a fair rate for their work. It makes for a difficult market. A growing part of my work and my firm's profits is simply connecting ZeroMQ users who want help with experts from the community able to provide it, and ensuring both sides are happy with the results.

I've seen communities of brilliant people with noble goals dying because the founders got some or all of these four things wrong. The core problem is that you can't expect consistently great leadership from any one company, person, or group. What works today often won't work tomorrow, yet structures become more solid, not more flexible, over time.

The best answer I can find is a mix of two things. One, the GPL and its guarantee of remixability. No matter how bad the authority, no matter how much they try to privatize and capture the community's work, if it's GPL licensed, that work can walk away and find a better authority. Before you say, "all open source offers this," think it through. I can kill a BSD-licensed project by hiring the core contributors and not releasing any new patches. But even with a billion of dollars, I *cannot* kill a GPL-licensed project. Two, the philosophical anarchist model of authority, which is that we choose it, it does not own us.

Chapter 4. The ZeroMQ Process: C4

When we say ZeroMQ we sometimes mean libzmq, the core library. In early 2012, we synthesized the libzmq process into a formal and *reusable* protocol for collaboration that we called the Collective Code Construction Contract[26], or C4. You can see this as a layer above the license (e.g. MPLv2). These are our rules, and I'll explain the reasoning behind each one.

C4 is an evolution of the GitHub Fork + Pull Model[27]. You may get the feeling I'm a fan of git and GitHub. This would be accurate: these two tools have made such a positive impact on our work over the last years, especially when it comes to building community.

Language

The key words "MUST", "MUST NOT", "REQUIRED", "SHALL", "SHALL NOT", "SHOULD", "SHOULD NOT", "RECOMMENDED", "MAY", and "OPTIONAL" in this document are to be interpreted as described in RFC 2119.

By starting with the RFC 2119 language, the C4 text makes very clear its intention to act as a protocol rather than a randomly written set of recommendations. A protocol is a contract between parties that defines the rights and obligations of each party. These can be peers in a network or they can be strangers working in the same project.

I think C4 is the first time anyone has attempted to codify a community's rulebook as a formal and reusable protocol spec. Previously, our rules were spread out over several wiki pages, and were quite specific to libzmq in many ways. But experience teaches us that the more formal, accurate, and reusable the rules, the easier it is for strangers to

---

26   http://rfc.zeromq.org/spec:42

27   http://help.github.com/send-pull-requests/

collaborate up-front. And less friction means a more scalable community. At the time of C4, we also had some disagreement in the libzmq project over precisely what process we were using. Not everyone felt bound by the same rules. Let's just say some people felt they had a special status, which created friction with the rest of the community. So codification made things clear.

It's easy to use C4: just host your project on GitHub, get one other person to join, and open the floor to pull requests. In your README, put a link to C4 and that's it. We've done this in quite a few projects and it does seem to work. I've been pleasantly surprised a few times just applying these rules to my own work, like CZMQ. None of us are so amazing that we can work without others.

Goals

C4 is meant to provide a reusable optimal collaboration model for open source software projects.

The short term reason for writing C4 was to end arguments over the libzmq contribution process. The dissenters went off elsewhere. The ZeroMQ community blossomed[28] smoothly and easily, as I'd predicted. Most people were surprised, but gratified. There's been no real criticisms of C4 except its branching policy, which I'll come to later as it deserves its own discussion.

There's a reason I'm reviewing history here: as founder of a community, you are asking people to invest in your property, trademark, and branding. In return, and this is what we do with ZeroMQ, you can use that branding to set a bar for quality. When you download a product labeled "ZeroMQ", you know that it's been produced to certain standards. It's a basic rule of quality: write down your process; otherwise you cannot improve it. Our processes aren't perfect, nor can they ever be. But any flaw in them can be fixed, and tested.

---

28 https://github.com/zeromq/libzmq/graphs/contributors

Making C4 reusable is therefore really important. To learn more about the best possible process, we need to get results from the widest range of projects.

It has these specific goals:

To maximize the scale of the community around a project, by reducing the friction for new Contributors and creating a scaled participation model with strong positive feedbacks;

The number one goal is size and health of the community—not technical quality, not profits, not performance, not market share. The goal is simply the number of people who contribute to the project. The science here is simple: the larger the community, the more accurate the results.

To relieve dependencies on key individuals by separating different skill sets so that there is a larger pool of competence in any required domain;

Perhaps the worst problem we faced in libzmq was dependence on people who could understand the code, manage GitHub branches, and make clean releases—all at the same time. It's like looking for athletes who can run marathons and sprint, swim, and also lift weights. We humans are really good at specialization. Asking us to be really good at two contradictory things reduces the number of candidates sharply, which is a Bad Thing for any project. We had this problem severely in libzmq in 2009 or so, and fixed it by splitting the role of maintainer into two: one person makes patches and another makes releases.

To allow the project to develop faster and more accurately, by increasing the diversity of the decision making process;

This is theory—not fully proven, but not falsified. The diversity of the community and the number of people who can weigh in on discussions, without fear of being criticized or dismissed, the faster and more accurately the software develops. Speed is quite subjective here.

Going very fast in the wrong direction is not just useless, it's actively damaging (and we suffered a lot of that in libzmq before we switched to C4).

To support the natural life cycle of project versions from experimental through to stable, by allowing safe experimentation, rapid failure, and isolation of stable code;

It's quite an interesting effect of the process: *the git master is almost always perfectly stable.* This has to do with the size of changes and their *latency,* i.e., the time between someone writing the code and someone actually using it fully. However, the healthy design learning process tends to cycle through drafts until becoming stable, and inviolable.

To reduce the internal complexity of project repositories, thus making it easier for Contributors to participate and reducing the scope for error;

Curious observation: people who thrive in complex situations like to create complexity because it keeps their value high. It's the Cobra Effect (Google it). Git made branches easy and left us with the all too common syndrome of "git is easy once you understand that a git branch is just a folded five-dimensional lepton space that has a detached history with no intervening cache". Developers should not be made to feel stupid by their tools. I've seen too many top-class developers confused by repository structures to accept conventional wisdom on git branches. We'll come back to dispose of git branches shortly, dear reader.

To enforce collective ownership of the project, which increases economic incentive to Contributors and reduces the risk of hijack by hostile entities.

Ultimately, we're economic creatures, and the sense that "we own this, and our work can never be used against us" makes it much easier for people to invest in an open source project like ZeroMQ. And it can't be just a feeling, it has to be real. There are a number of aspects to making collective ownership work, we'll see these one-by-one as we go through C4.

Preliminaries

The project SHALL use the git distributed revision control system.

Git has its faults. Its command-line API is horribly inconsistent, and it has a complex, messy internal model that it shoves in your face at the slightest provocation. But despite doing its best to make its users feel stupid, git does its job really, really well. More pragmatically, I've found that if you stay away from certain areas (branches!), people learn git rapidly and don't make many mistakes. That works for me.

The project SHALL be hosted on github.com or equivalent, herein called the "Platform".

I'm sure one day some large firm will buy GitHub and break it, and another platform will rise in its place. Until then, Github serves up a near-perfect set of minimal, fast, simple tools. I've thrown hundreds of people at it, and they all stick like flies stuck in a dish of honey.

The project SHALL use the Platform issue tracker.

We made the mistake in libzmq of switching to Jira because we hadn't learned yet how to properly use the GitHub issue tracker. Jira is a great example of how to turn something useful into a complex mess because the business depends on selling more "features". But even without criticizing Jira, keeping the issue tracker on the same platform means one less UI to learn, one less login, and smooth integration between issues and patches.

The project SHOULD have clearly documented guidelines for code style.

This is a protocol plug-in: insert code style guidelines here. If you don't document the code style you use, you have no basis except prejudice to reject patches.

A "Contributor" is a person who wishes to provide a patch, being a set of commits that solve some clearly identified problem.

A "Maintainer" is a person who merge patches to the project. Maintainers are not developers; their job is to enforce process.

Now we move on to definitions of the parties, and the splitting of roles that saved us from the sin of structural dependency on rare individuals. This worked well in libzmq, but as you will see it depends on the rest of the process. C4 isn't a buffet; you will need the whole process (or something very like it), or it won't hold together.

Contributors SHALL NOT have commit access to the repository unless they are also Maintainers.

Maintainers SHALL have commit access to the repository.

What we wanted to avoid was people pushing their changes directly to master. This was the biggest source of trouble in libzmq historically: large masses of raw code that took months or years to fully stabilize. We eventually followed other ZeroMQ projects like PyZMQ in using pull requests. We went further, and stipulated that *all* changes had to follow the same path. No exceptions for "special people".

Everyone, without distinction or discrimination, SHALL have an equal right to become a Contributor under the terms of this contract.

We had to state this explicitly. It used to be that the libzmq maintainers would reject patches simply because they didn't like them. Now, that may sound reasonable to the author of a library (though libzmq was not written by any one person), but let's remember our goal of creating a work that is owned by as many people as possible. Saying "I don't like your patch so I'm going to reject it" is equivalent to saying, "I claim to own this and I think I'm better than you, and I don't trust you". Those are toxic messages to give to others who are thinking of becoming your co-investors.

I think this fight between individual expertise and collective intelligence plays out in other areas. It defined Wikipedia, and still does, a decade after that work surpassed anything built by small groups of experts. For me, we make software by slowly synthesizing the most accurate knowledge, much as we make Wikipedia articles.

Licensing and Ownership

The project SHALL use a share-alike license such as the MPLv2, or a GPLv3 variant thereof (GPL, LGPL, AGPL).

I've already explained how full remixability creates better scale and why MPLv2 or GPL and its variants seems the optimal contract for remixable software. If you're a large business aiming to dump code on the market, you won't want C4, but then you won't really care about community either.

All contributions to the project source code ("patches") SHALL use the same license as the project.

This removes the need for any specific license or contribution agreement for patches. You fork the MPLv2 or GPL code, you publish your remixed version on GitHub, and you or anyone else can then submit that as a patch to the original code. BSD doesn't allow this. Any work that contains BSD code may also contain unlicensed proprietary code so you need explicit action from the author of the code before you can remix it.

All patches are owned by their authors. There SHALL NOT be any copyright assignment process.

Here we come to the key reason people trust their investments in ZeroMQ: it's logistically impossible to buy the copyrights to create a closed source competitor to ZeroMQ. iMatix can't do this either. And the more people that send patches, the harder it becomes. ZeroMQ isn't just free and open today—this specific rule means it will remain so forever. Note that it's not the case in all MPLv2/GPL projects, many of which still ask for copyright transfer back to the maintainers.

Each Contributor SHALL be responsible for identifying themselves in the project Contributor list.

In other words, the maintainers are not karma accountants. Anyone who wants credit has to claim it themselves.

Patch Requirements

In this section, we define the obligations of the contributor: specifically, what constitutes a "valid" patch, so that maintainers have rules they can use to accept or reject patches.

Maintainers and Contributors MUST have a Platform account and SHOULD use their real names or a well-known alias.

In the worst case scenario, where someone has submitted toxic code (patented, or owned by someone else), we need to be able to trace who and when, so we can remove the code. Asking for real names or a well-known alias is a theoretical strategy for reducing the risk of bogus patches. We don't know if this actually works because we haven't had the problem yet.

A patch SHOULD be a minimal and accurate answer to exactly one identified and agreed problem.

This implements the Simplicity Oriented Design process that I'll come to later in this chapter. One clear problem, one minimal solution, apply, test, repeat.

A patch MUST adhere to the code style guidelines of the project if these are defined.

This is just sanity. I've spent time cleaning up other peoples' patches because they insisted on putting the else beside the if instead of just below as Nature intended. Consistent code is healthier.

A patch MUST adhere to the "Evolution of Public Contracts" guidelines defined below.

Ah, the pain, the pain. I'm not speaking of the time at age eight when I stepped on a plank with a 4-inch nail protruding from it. That was relatively OK. I'm speaking of 2010-2011 when we had multiple parallel releases of ZeroMQ, each with different *incompatible* APIs or wire protocols. It was an exercise in bad rules, pointlessly enforced, that still hurts us today. The rule was, "If you change the API or pro-tocol, you SHALL create a new major version". Give me the nail through the foot; that hurt less.

One of the big changes we made with C4 was simply to ban, out-right, this kind of sanctioned sabotage. Amazingly, it's not even hard. We just don't allow the breaking of existing public contracts, period, unless everyone agrees, in which case no period. As Linus Torvalds famously put it on 23 December 2012, "WE DO NOT BREAK USERSPACE!"

A patch SHALL NOT include nontrivial code from other projects unless the Contributor is the original author of that code.

This rule has two effects. The first is that it forces people to make minimal solutions because they cannot simply import swathes of ex-isting code. In the cases where I've seen this happen to projects, it's al-ways bad unless the imported code is very cleanly separated. The second is that it avoids license arguments. You write the patch, you are allowed to publish it as LGPL, and we can merge it back in. But you find a 200-line code fragment on the web, and try to paste that, we'll refuse.

A patch MUST compile cleanly and pass project self-tests on at least the principle target platform.

For cross-platform projects, it is fair to ask that the patch works on the development box used by the contributor.

* A patch commit message MUST consist of a single short (less than 50 characters) line stating the problem ("Problem: ...")

being solved, followed by a blank line and then the proposed solution ("Solution: ...").

This is a good format for commit messages that fits into email (the first line becomes the subject, and the rest becomes the email body).

A "Correct Patch" is one that satisfies the above requirements.

Just in case it wasn't clear, we're back to legalese and definitions.

Development Process

In this section, we aim to describe the actual development process, step-by-step.

Change on the project SHALL be governed by the pattern of accurately identifying problems and applying minimal, accurate solutions to these problems.

This is a unapologetic ramming through of thirty years' software design experience. It's a profoundly simple approach to design: make minimal, accurate solutions to real problems, nothing more or less. In ZeroMQ, we don't have feature requests. Treating new features the same as bugs confuses some newcomers. But this process works, and not just in open source. Enunciating the problem we're trying to solve, with every single change, is key to deciding whether the change is worth making or not.

To request changes, a user SHOULD log an issue on the project Platform issue tracker.

This is how users talk to contributors. Track your problems, so others can (maybe) try to solve them for you.

The user or Contributor SHOULD write the issue by describing the problem they face or observe.

"Problem: we need feature X. Solution: make it" is not a good issue. "Problem: user cannot do common tasks A or B except by using a complex workaround. Solution: make feature X" is a decent explanation. Because everyone I've ever worked with has needed to learn this, it seems worth restating: document the real problem first, solution second.

The user or Contributor SHOULD seek consensus on the accuracy of their observation, and the value of solving the problem.

And because many apparent problems are illusionary, by stating the problem explicitly we give others a chance to correct our logic. "You're only using A and B a lot because function C is unreliable. Solution: make function C work properly."

Users SHALL NOT log feature requests, ideas, suggestions, or any solutions to problems that are not explicitly documented and provable.

There are several reasons for not logging ideas, suggestions, or feature requests. In our experience, these just accumulate in the issue tracker until someone deletes them. But more profoundly, when we treat all change as problem solutions, we can prioritize trivially. Either the problem is real and someone wants to solve it now, or it's not on the table. Thus, wish lists are off the table.

Thus, the release history of the project SHALL be a list of meaningful issues logged and solved.

I'd love the GitHub issue tracker to simply list all the issues we solved in each release. Today we still have to write that by hand. If one puts the issue number in each commit, and if one uses the GitHub issue tracker, which we sadly don't yet do for ZeroMQ, this release history is easier to produce mechanically.

To work on an issue, a Contributor SHALL fork the project repository and then work on their forked repository.

Here we explain the GitHub fork + pull request model so that newcomers only have to learn one process (C4) in order to contribute.

To submit a patch, a Contributor SHALL create a Platform pull request back to the project.

GitHub has made this so simple that we don't need to learn git commands to do it, for which I'm deeply grateful. Sometimes, I'll tell people who I don't particularly like that command-line git is awesome and all they need to do is learn git's internal model in detail before trying to use it on real work. When I see them several months later they look... changed.

A Contributor SHALL NOT commit changes directly to the project.

Anyone who submits a patch is a contributor, and all contributors follow the same rules. No special privileges to the original authors, because otherwise we're not building a community, only boosting our egos.

To discuss a patch, people MAY comment on the Platform pull request, on the commit, or elsewhere.

Randomly distributed discussions may be confusing if you're walking up for the first time, but GitHub solves this for all current participants by sending emails to those who need to follow what's going on. We had the same experience and the same solution in Wikidot, and it works. There's no evidence that discussing in different places has any negative effect.

To accept or reject a patch, a Maintainer SHALL use the Platform interface.

Working via the GitHub web user interface means pull requests are logged as issues, with workflow and discussion. I'm sure there are more complex ways to work. Complexity is easy; it's simplicity that's incredibly hard.

Maintainers SHALL NOT accept their own patches.

There was a rule we defined in the FFII years ago to stop people burning out: no less than two people on any project. One-person projects tend to end in tears, or at least bitter silence. We have quite a lot of data on burnout, why it happens, and how to prevent it (even cure it). I'll explore this later in the chapter, because if you work with or on open source you need to be aware of the risks. The "no merging your own patch" rule has two goals. First, if you want your project to be C4-certified, you have to get at least one other person to help. If no one wants to help you, perhaps you need to rethink your project. Second, having a control for every patch makes it much more satisfying, keeps us more focused, and stops us breaking the rules because we're in a hurry, or just feeling lazy.

Maintainers SHALL NOT make value judgments on correct patches.

We already said this but it's worth repeating: the role of Maintainer is not to judge a patch's substance, only its technical quality. The substantive worth of a patch only emerges over time: people use it, and like it, or they do not. And if no one is using a patch, eventually it'll annoy someone else who will remove it, and no one will complain.

Maintainers SHALL merge correct patches rapidly.

There is a criteria I call *change latency*, which is the round-trip time from identifying a problem to testing a solution. The faster the better. If maintainers cannot respond to pull requests as rapidly as people expect, they're not doing their job (or they need more hands).

Maintainers MAY merge incorrect patches from other Contributors with the goals of (a) ending fruitless discussions, (b) capturing toxic patches in the historical record, (c) engaging with the Contributor on improving their patch quality.

It turns out that accepting imperfect patches rapidly, which I call "optimistic merging", works better all-round than insisting that contributors deliver perfect work.

Standard practice (Pessimistic Merging, or PM) is to wait until continuous integration testing (CI) is done, then do a code review, then test the patch on a branch, and then provide feedback to the author. The author can then fix the patch and the test/review cycle starts again. At this stage the maintainer can (and often does) make value judgments such as "I don't like how you do this" or "this doesn't fit with our project vision."

In the worst case, patches can wait for weeks, or months, to be accepted. Or they are never accepted. Or, they are rejected with various excuses and argumentation.

PM is how most projects work, and I believe most projects get it wrong. Let me start by listing the problems PM creates:

- *It tells new contributors, "guilty until proven innocent,"* which is a negative message that creates negative emotions. Contributors who feel unwelcome will always look for alternatives. Driving away contributors is bad. Making slow, quiet enemies is worse.

- *It gives maintainers power over new contributors*, which many maintainers abuse. This abuse can be subconscious. Yet it is widespread. Maintainers inherently strive to remain important in their project. If they can keep out potential competitors by delaying and blocking their patches, they will.

- *It opens the door to discrimination.* One can argue, a project belongs to its maintainers, so they can choose who they want to work with. My response is: projects that are not aggressively inclusive will die, and deserve to die.

- *It slows down the learning cycle.* Innovation demands rapid experiment-failure-success cycles. Someone identifies a problem or inefficiency in a product. Someone proposes a fix. The fix is tested and works or fails. We have learned something new. The faster this cycle happens, the faster and more accurately the project can move.

- *It gives outsiders the chance to troll the project.* It is a simple as raising an objection to a new patch. "I don't like this code." Discussions over details can use up much more effort than writing code. It is far cheaper to attack a patch than to make one. These economics favor the trolls and punish the honest contributors.

- *It puts the burden of work on individual contributors,* which is ironic and sad for open source. We want to work together yet we're told to fix our work alone.

Now let's see how this works when we use Optimistic Merging, or OM. To start with, understand that not all patches nor all contributors are the same. We see at least four main cases in our open source projects:

1. Good contributors who know the rules and write excellent, perfect patches.

2. Good contributors who make mistakes, and who write useful yet broken patches.

3. Mediocre contributors who make patches that no-one notices or cares about.

4. Trollish contributors who ignore the rules, and who write toxic patches.

PM assumes all patches are toxic until proven good (4). Whereas in reality most patches tend to be useful, and worth improving (2).

Let's see how each scenario works, with PM and OM:

1. PM: depending on unspecified, arbitrary criteria, patch may be merged rapidly or slowly. At least sometimes, a good contributor will be left with bad feelings. OM: good contributors feel happy and appreciated, and continue to provide excellent patches until they are done using the project.

2. PM: contributor retreats, fixes patch, comes back somewhat humiliated. OM: second contributor joins in to help first fix their patch. We get a short, happy patch party. New contributor now has a coach and friend in the project.

3. PM: we get a flamewar and everyone wonders why the community is so hostile. OM: the mediocre contributor is largely ignored. If patch needs fixing, it'll happen rapidly. Contributor loses interest and eventually the patch is reverted.

4. PM: we get a flamewar which troll wins by sheer force of argument. Community explodes in fight-or-flee emotions. Bad patches get pushed through. OM: existing contributor immediately reverts the patch. There is no discussion. Troll may try again, and eventually may be banned. Toxic patches remain in git history forever.

In each case, OM has a better outcome than PM.

In the majority case (patches that need further work), Optimistic Merging creates the conditions for mentoring and coaching. And indeed this is what we see in ZeroMQ projects, and is one of the reasons they are such fun to work on.

The user who created an issue SHOULD close the issue after checking the patch is successful.

When one person opens an issue, and another works on it, it's best to allow the original person to close the issue. That acts as a double-check that the issue was properly resolved.

Any Contributor who has value judgments on a patch SHOULD express these via their own patches.

In essence, the goal here is to allow users to try patches rather than to spend time arguing pros and cons. As easy as it is to make a patch, it's as easy to revert it with another patch. You might think this would lead to "patch wars", but that hasn't happened. We've had a handful of cases in libzmq where patches by one contributor were killed by another person who felt the experimentation wasn't going in the right direction. It is easier than seeking up-front consensus.

Maintainers SHOULD close user issues that are left open without action for an uncomfortable period of time.

Just keep the issue tracker clean.

Branches and Releases

When C4 is working, we get two massive simplifications of our delivery process. One, we don't need or use branches. Two, we deliver from master.

This is the process we explain in this section.

The project SHALL have one branch ("master") that always holds the latest in-progress version and SHOULD always build.

This is redundant because every patch always builds but it's worth restating. If the master doesn't build (and pass its tests), someone needs waking up.

The project SHALL NOT use topic branches for any reason. Personal forks MAY use topic branches.

I'll come to branches soon. In short (or "tl;dr", as they say on the webs), branches make the repository too complex and fragile, and require up-front agreement, all of which are expensive and avoidable.

To make a stable release a Maintainer shall tag the repository. Stable releases SHALL always be released from the repository master.

Evolution of Public Contracts

By "public contracts", I mean APIs and protocols. Up until the end of 2011, libzmq's naturally happy state was marred by broken promises and broken contracts. We stopped making promises (aka "road maps") for libzmq completely, and our dominant theory of change is now that it emerges carefully and accurately over time. At a 2012 Chicago meetup, Garrett Smith and Chuck Remes called this the "drunken stumble to greatness", which is how I think of it now.

We stopped breaking public contracts simply by banning the practice. Before then it had been "OK" (as in we did it and everyone complained bitterly, and we ignored them) to break the API or protocol so long as we changed the major version number. Sounds fine, until you get ZeroMQ v2.0, v3.0, and v4.0 all in development at the same time, and not speaking to each other.

All Public Contracts (APIs or protocols) SHALL be documented.

You'd think this was a given for professional software engineers but no, it's not. So, it's a rule. You want C4 certification for your project, you make sure your public contracts are documented. No "It's specified in the code" excuses. Code is not a contract. (Yes, I intend at some point to create a C4 certification process to act as a quality indicator for open source projects.)

All Public Contracts SHOULD have space for extensibility and experimentation.

Now, the real thing is that public contracts *do change*. It's not about not changing them. It's about changing them safely. This means educating (especially protocol) designers to create that space up-front.

A patch that modifies a stable Public Contract SHOULD not break existing applications unless there is overriding consensus on the value of doing this.

Sometimes the patch is fixing a bad API that no one is using. It's a freedom we need, but it should be based on consensus, not one person's dogma. However, making random changes "just because" is not good. In ZeroMQ v3.x, did we benefit from renaming ZMQ_NOBLOCK to ZMQ_DONTWAIT? Sure, it's closer to the POSIX socket recv() call, but is that worth breaking thousands of applications? No one ever reported it as an issue. To misquote Stallman: "your freedom to create an ideal world stops one inch from my application."

A patch that introduces new features SHOULD do so using new names (a new contract).

We had the experience in ZeroMQ once or twice of new features using old names (or worse, using names that were *still in use* elsewhere). ZeroMQ v3.0 had a newly introduced "ROUTER" socket that was totally different from the existing ROUTER socket in 2.x. Dear lord, you should be face-palming, why? The reason: apparently, even smart people sometimes need regulation to stop them doing silly things.

New contracts SHOULD be marked as "draft" until they are stable and used by real users.

Old contracts SHOULD be deprecated in a systematic fashion by marking new contracts as "draft" until they are stable, then marking the old contracts as "deprecated".

This life cycle notation has the great benefit of actually telling users what is going on with a consistent direction. "Draft" means "we have introduced this and intend to make it stable if it works". It does not mean, "we have introduced this and will remove it at any time if we feel like it". One assumes that code that survives more than one patch cycle is meant to be there. "Deprecated" means "we have replaced this and intend to remove it".

Old contracts SHOULD be deprecated in a systematic fashion by marking them as "deprecated" and replacing them with new contracts as needed.

When sufficient time has passed, old deprecated contracts SHOULD be removed.

In theory this gives applications time to move onto stable new contracts without risk. You can upgrade first, make sure things work, and then, over time, fix things up to remove dependencies on deprecated and legacy APIs and protocols.

Old names SHALL NOT be reused by new features.

Ah, yes, the joy when ZeroMQ v3.x renamed the top-used API functions (`zmq_send[3]` and `zmq_recv[3]`) and then recycled the old names for new methods that were utterly incompatible (and which I suspect few people actually use). You should be slapping yourself in confusion again, but really, this is what happened and I was as guilty as anyone. After all, we did change the version number! The only benefit of that experience was to get this rule.

Project Administration

The project founders SHALL act as Administrators to manage the set of project Maintainers.

Someone needs to administer the project, and it makes sense that the original founders start this ball rolling.

The Administrators SHALL ensure their own succession over time by promoting the most effective Maintainers.

At the same time, as founder of a project you really want to get out of the way before you become over-attached to it. Promoting the most active and consistent maintainers is good for everyone.

A new Contributor who makes correct patches, who clearly understands the project goals, and the process SHOULD be invited to become a Maintainer.

Promote your contributors rapidly, when they show they get it. Anything else is counter-productive.

Administrators SHOULD remove Maintainers who are inactive for an extended period of time, or who repeatedly fail to apply this process accurately.

This was Ian Barber's suggestion: we need a way to crop inactive maintainers. Originally maintainers were self-elected but that makes it hard to drop troublemakers (who are rare, but not unknown).

Administrators SHOULD block or ban "bad actors" who cause stress and pain to others in the project. This should be done after public discussion, with a chance for all parties to speak. A bad actor is someone who repeatedly ignores the rules and culture of the project, who is needlessly argumentative or hostile, or who is offensive, and who is unable to self-correct their behavior when asked to do so by others.

Now and then, your projects will attract people of the wrong character. You will get better at seeing these people, over time. C4 helps in two ways. One, by setting out strong rules, it discourages the chaos-seekers and bullies, who cannot tolerate others' rules. Two, it gives you the Administrator the power to ban them. I like to give such people time, to show themselves, and get their patches on the public record (a reason to merge bad patches, which of course you can remove after a suitable pause).

Chapter 5. Designing for Innovation

Let's look at innovation, which Wikipedia defines as, "the development of new values through solutions that meet new requirements, inarticulate needs, or old customer and market needs in value adding new ways." This really just means solving problems more cheaply. It sounds straight-forward, but the history of collapsed tech giants proves that it's not. I'll try to explain how teams so often get it wrong, and suggest a way for doing innovation right.

The Tale of Two Bridges

Two old engineers were talking of their lives and boasting of their greatest projects. One of the engineers explained how he had designed one of the greatest bridges ever made.

"We built it across a river gorge," he told his friend. "It was wide and deep. We spent two years studying the land, and choosing designs and materials. We hired the best engineers and designed the bridge, which took another five years. We contracted the largest engineering firms to build the structures, the towers, the tollbooths, and the roads that would connect the bridge to the main highways. Dozens died during the construction. Under the road level we had trains, and a special path for cyclists. That bridge represented years of my life."

The second man reflected for a while, then spoke. "One evening me and a friend got drunk on vodka, and we threw a rope across a gorge," he said. "Just a rope, tied to two trees. There were two villages, one at each side. At first, people pulled packages across that rope with a pulley and string. Then someone threw a second rope, and built a foot walk. It was dangerous, but the kids loved it. A group of men then re-built that, made it solid, and women started to cross, everyday, with their produce. A market grew up on one side of the bridge, and slowly that became a large town, because there was a lot of space for houses. The rope bridge got replaced with a wooden bridge, to allow horses and carts to cross. Then the town built a real stone bridge, with metal beams. Later, they replaced the stone part with steel, and today there's a suspension bridge standing in that same spot."

The first engineer was silent. "Funny thing," he said, "my bridge was demolished about ten years after we built it. Turns out it was built in the wrong place and no one wanted to use it. Some guys had thrown a rope across the gorge, a few miles further downstream, and that's where everyone went."

How ZeroMQ Lost Its Road Map

Presenting ZeroMQ at the Mix-IT conference in Lyon in early 2012, I was asked several times for the "road map". My answer was: there is no road map any longer. We had road maps, and we deleted them. Instead of a few experts trying to lay out the next steps, we were allowing this to happen organically. The audience didn't really like my answer. So un-French.

However, the history of ZeroMQ makes it quite clear why road maps were problematic. In the beginning, we had a small team making the library, with few contributors, and no documented road map. As ZeroMQ grew more popular and we switched to more contributors, users asked for road maps. So we collected our plans together and tried to organize them into releases. Here, we wrote, is what will come in the next release.

As we rolled out releases, we hit the problem that it's very easy to promise stuff, and rather harder to make it as planned. For one thing, much of the work was voluntary, and it's not clear how you force volunteers to commit to a road map. But also, priorities can shift dramatically over time. So we were making promises we could not keep, and the real deliveries didn't match the road maps.

The second problem was that by defining the road map, we in effect claimed territory, making it harder for others to participate. People do prefer to contribute to changes they believe were their idea. Writing down a list of things to do turns contribution into a chore rather than an opportunity.

Finally, we saw changes in ZeroMQ that were quite traumatic, and the road maps didn't help with this, despite a lot of discussion and effort to "do it right". Examples of this were incompatible changes in APIs and protocols. It was quite clear that we needed a different approach for defining the change process.

Software engineers don't like the notion that powerful, effective solutions can come into existence without an intelligent designer actively thinking things through. And yet no one in that room in Lyon would have questioned evolution. A strange irony, and one I wanted to explore further as it underpins the direction the ZeroMQ community has taken since the start of 2012.

In the dominant theory of innovation, brilliant individuals reflect on large problem sets and then carefully and precisely create a solution. Sometimes they will have "eureka" moments where they "get" brilliantly simple answers to whole large problem sets. The inventor, and the process of invention are rare, precious, and can command a monopoly. History is full of such heroic individuals. We owe them our modern world.

Looking more closely, however, and you will see that the facts don't match. History doesn't show lone inventors. It shows lucky people who steal or claim ownership of ideas that are being worked on by many. It shows brilliant people striking lucky once, and then spending decades on fruitless and pointless quests. The best known large-scale inventors like Thomas Edison were in fact just very good at systematic broad research done by large teams. It's like claiming that Steve Jobs invented every device made by Apple. It is a nice myth, good for marketing, but utterly useless as practical science.

Recent history, much better documented and less easy to manipulate, shows this well. The Internet is surely one of the most innovative and fast-moving areas of technology, and one of the best documented. It has no inventor. Instead, it has a massive economy of people who have carefully and progressively solved a long series of immediate problems, documented their answers, and made those available to all. The innovative nature of the Internet comes not from a small, select band of Einsteins. It comes from RFCs anyone can use and improve, made by hundreds and thousands of smart, but not uniquely smart, individuals. It comes from open source software anyone can use and improve. It comes from sharing, scale of community, and the continuous accretion of good solutions and disposal of bad ones.

Here thus is an alternative theory of innovation:

1. There is an infinite problem/solution terrain.

2. This terrain changes over time according to external conditions.

3. We can only accurately perceive problems to which we are close.

4. We can rank the cost/benefit economics of problems using a market for solutions.

5. There is an optimal solution to any solvable problem.

6. We can approach this optimal solution heuristically, and mechanically.

7. Our intelligence can make this process faster, but does not replace it.

There are a few corollaries to this:

- *Individual creativity matters less than process.* Smarter people may work faster, but they may also work in the wrong direction. It's the collective vision of reality that keeps us honest and relevant.

- *We don't need road maps if we have a good process.* Functionality will emerge and evolve over time as solutions compete for market share.

- *We don't invent solutions so much as discover them.* All sympathies to the creative soul. It's just an information processing machine that likes to polish its own ego and collect karma.

- *Intelligence is a social effect, though it feels personal.* A person cut off from others eventually stops thinking. We can neither collect problems nor measure solutions without other people.
- *The size and diversity of the community is a key factor.* Larger, more diverse communities collect more relevant problems, and solve them more accurately, and do this faster, than a small expert group.

So, when we trust the solitary experts, they make classic mistakes. They focus on ideas, not problems. They focus on the wrong problems. They make misjudgments about the value of solving problems. They don't use their own work.

Can we turn the above theory into a reusable process? In late 2011, I started documenting C4 and similar contracts, and using them both in ZeroMQ and in closed source projects. The underlying process is something I call "Simplicity Oriented Design", or SOD. This is a reproducible way of developing simple and elegant products. It organizes people into flexible supply chains that are able to navigate a problem landscape rapidly and cheaply. They do this by building, testing, and keeping or discarding minimal plausible solutions, called "patches". Living products consist of long series of patches, applied one atop the other.

SOD is relevant first because it's how we evolve ZeroMQ. It's also the basis for the design process we use to develop larger-scale ZeroMQ applications. Of course, you can use any software architecture methodology with ZeroMQ.

To best understand how we ended up with SOD, let's look at the alternatives.

Trash-Oriented Design

The most popular design process in large businesses seems to be *Trash-Oriented Design*, or TOD. TOD feeds off the belief that all we need to make money are great ideas. It's tenacious nonsense, but a powerful crutch for people who lack imagination. The theory goes that ideas are rare, so the trick is to capture them. It's like non-musicians being awed by a guitar player, not realizing that great talent is so cheap it literally plays on the streets for coins.

The main output of TODs is expensive "ideation": concepts, design documents, and products that go straight into the trash can. It works as follows:

- The Creative People come up with long lists of "we could do X and Y". I've seen endlessly detailed lists of everything amazing a product could do. We've all been guilty of this. Once the creative work of idea generation has happened, it's just a matter of execution, of course.

- So the managers and their consultants pass their brilliant ideas to designers who create acres of preciously refined design documents. The designers take the tens of ideas the managers came up with, and turn them into hundreds of world-changing designs.

- These designs get given to engineers who scratch their heads and wonder who the heck came up with such nonsense. They start to argue back, but the designs come from up high, and really, it's not up to engineers to argue with creative people and expensive consultants.

- So the engineers creep back to their cubicles, humiliated and threatened into building the gigantic but oh-so-elegant junk heap. It is bone-breaking work because the designs take no account of practical costs. Minor whims might take weeks of work to build. As the project gets delayed, the managers bully the engineers into giving up their evenings and weekends.

- Eventually, something resembling a working product makes it out of the door. It's creaky and fragile, complex and ugly. The designers curse the engineers for their incompetence and pay more consultants to put lipstick onto the pig, and slowly the product starts to look a little nicer.

- By this time, the managers have started to try to sell the product and they find, shockingly, that no one wants it. Undaunted, they courageously build million-dollar web sites and ad campaigns to explain to the public why they absolutely need this product. They do deals with other businesses to force the product on the lazy, stupid, and ungrateful market.

- After twelve months of intense marketing, the product still isn't making profits. Worse, it suffers dramatic failures and gets branded in the press as a disaster. The company quietly shelves it, fires the consultants, buys a competing product from a small startup and rebrands that as its own Version 2. Hundreds of millions of dollars end up in the trash.

- Meanwhile, another visionary manager somewhere in the organization drinks a little too much tequila with some marketing people and has a Brilliant Idea.

Trash-Oriented Design would be a caricature if it wasn't so common. Something like 19 out of 20 market-ready products built by large firms are failures (yes, 87% of statistics are made up on the spot). The remaining 1 in 20 probably only succeeds because the competitors are so bad and the marketing is so aggressive.

The main lessons of TOD are quite straightforward but hard to swallow. They are:

- Ideas are cheap. No exceptions. There are no brilliant ideas. Anyone who tries to start a discussion with "oooh, we can do this too!" should be beaten down with all the passion one reserves for traveling evangelists. It is like sitting in a cafe at the foot of a mountain, drinking a hot chocolate and telling others, "Hey, I have a great idea, we can climb that mountain! And build a chalet on top! With two saunas! And a garden! Hey, and we can make it solar powered! Dude, that's awesome! What color should we paint it? Green! No, blue! OK, go and make it, I'll stay here and make spreadsheets and graphics!"

- The starting point for a good design process is to collect real problems that confront real people. The second step is to evaluate these problems with the basic question, "How much is it worth to solve this problem?" Having done that, we can collect that set of problems that are worth solving.

- Good solutions to real problems will succeed as products. Their success will depend on how good and cheap the solution is, and how important the problem is (and sadly, how big the marketing budgets are). But their success will also depend on how much they demand in effort to use—in other words, how simple they are.

Now, after slaying the dragon of utter irrelevance, we attack the demon of complexity.

Complexity-Oriented Design

Really good engineering teams and small firms can usually build decent products. But the vast majority of products still end up being too complex and less successful than they might be. This is because specialist teams, even the best, often stubbornly apply a process I call *Complexity-Oriented Design*, or COD, which works as follows:

- Management correctly identifies some interesting and difficult problem with economic value. In doing so, they already leapfrog over any TOD team.

- The team with enthusiasm starts to build prototypes and core layers. These work as designed and thus encouraged, the team go off into intense design and architecture discussions, coming up with elegant schemas that look beautiful and solid.

- Management comes back and challenges the team with yet more difficult problems. We tend to equate cost with value, so the harder and more expensive to solve, the more the solution should be worth, in their minds.

- The team, being engineers and thus loving to build stuff, build stuff. They build and build and build and end up with massive, perfectly-designed complexity.

- The products go to market, and the market scratches its head and asks, "Seriously, is this the best you can do?" People do use the products, especially if they aren't spending their own money in climbing the learning curve.

- Management gets positive feedback from its larger customers, who share the same idea that high cost (in training and use) means high value, and so continues to push the process.

- Meanwhile somewhere across the world, a small team is solving the same problem using a better process, and a year later smashes the market to little pieces.

COD is characterized by a team obsessively solving the wrong problems in a form of collective delusion. COD products tend to be large, ambitious, complex, and unpopular. Much open source software is the output of COD processes. It is insanely hard for engineers to *stop* extending a design to cover more potential problems. They argue, "What if someone wants to do X?" but never ask themselves, "What is the real value of solving X?"

A good example of COD in practice is Bluetooth, a complex, over-designed set of protocols that users hate. It continues to exist only because in a massively-patented industry there are no real alternatives. Bluetooth is perfectly secure, which is close to pointless for a proximity protocol. At the same time, it lacks a standard API for developers, meaning it's really costly to use Bluetooth in applications.

On the #zeromq IRC channel, Wintre once wrote of how enraged he was many years ago when he "found that XMMS 2 had a working plugin system, but could not actually play music."

COD is a form of large-scale "rabbit-holing", in which designers and engineers cannot distance themselves from the technical details of their work. They add more and more features, utterly misreading the economics of their work.

The main lessons of COD are also simple, but hard for experts to swallow. They are:

- Making stuff that you don't immediately have a need for is pointless. Doesn't matter how talented or brilliant you are, if you just

sit down and make stuff people are not actually asking for, you are
most likely wasting your time.

- Problems are not equal. Some are simple, and some are complex.
  Ironically, solving the simpler problems often has more value to
  more people than solving the really hard ones. So if you allow engineers to just work on random things, they'll mostly focus on the
  most interesting but least worthwhile things.

- Engineers and designers love to make stuff and decoration, and
  this inevitably leads to complexity. It is crucial to have a "stop
  mechanism", a way to set short, hard deadlines that force people
  to make smaller, simpler answers to just the most crucial problems.

Simplicity Oriented Design

Finally, we come to the rare but precious *Simplicity Oriented
Design*, or SOD. This process starts with a realization: we do not
know what we have to make until after we start making it. Coming up
with ideas or large-scale designs isn't just wasteful, it's a direct
hindrance to designing the truly accurate solutions. The really juicy
problems are hidden like far valleys, and any activity except active
scouting creates a fog that hides those distant valleys. You need to
keep mobile, pack light, and move fast.

SOD works as follows:

- We collect a set of interesting problems (by looking at how people
  use technology or other products) and we line these up from
  simple to complex, looking for and identifying patterns of use.

- We take the simplest, most dramatic problem and we solve this
  with a minimal plausible solution, or "patch". Each patch solves
  exactly a genuine and agreed-upon problem in a brutally minimal
  fashion.

- We apply one measure of quality to patches, namely "Can this be
  done any simpler while still solving the stated problem?" We can
  measure complexity in terms of concepts and models that the user

has to learn or guess in order to use the patch. The fewer, the better. A perfect patch solves a problem with zero learning required by the user.

- Our product development consists of a patch that solves the problem "we need a proof of concept" and then evolves in an unbroken line to a mature series of products, through hundreds or thousands of patches piled on top of each other.

- We do not do *anything* that is not a patch. We enforce this rule with formal processes that demand that every activity or task is tied to a genuine and agreed-upon problem, explicitly enunciated and documented.

- We build our projects into a supply chain where each project can provide problems to its "suppliers" and receive patches in return. The supply chain creates the "stop mechanism" because when people are impatiently waiting for an answer, we necessarily cut our work short.

- Individuals are free to work on any projects, and provide patches at any place they feel it's worthwhile. No individuals "own" any project, except to enforce the formal processes. A single project can have many variations, each a collection of different, competing patches.

- Projects export formal and documented interfaces so that upstream (client) projects are unaware of change happening in supplier projects. Thus multiple supplier projects can compete for client projects, in effect creating a free and competitive market.

- We tie our supply chain to real users and external clients and we drive the whole process by rapid cycles so that a problem received from outside users can be analyzed, evaluated, and solved with a patch in a few hours.

- At every moment from the very first patch, our product is shippable. This is essential, because a large proportion of patches will be wrong (10-30%) and only by giving the product to users can we know which patches have become problems that need solving.

SOD is a *hill-climbing algorithm*, a reliable way of finding optimal solutions to the most significant problems in an unknown landscape. You don't need to be a genius to use SOD successfully, you just need to be able to see the difference between the fog of activity and the progress towards new real problems.

People have pointed out that hill-climbing algorithms have known limitations. One gets stuck on local peaks, mainly. But this is nonetheless how life itself works: collecting tiny incremental improvements over long periods of time. There is no intelligent designer. We reduce the risk of local peaks by spreading out widely across the landscape, but it is somewhat moot. The limitations aren't optional, they are physical laws. The theory says, *this is how innovation really works, so better embrace it and work with it than try to work on the basis of magical thinking.*

And in fact once you see all innovation as more or less successful hill-climbing, you realize why some teams and companies and products get stuck in a never-never land of diminishing prospects. They simply don't have the diversity and collective intelligence to find better hills to climb. When Nokia killed their open source projects, they cut their own throat.

A really good designer with a good team can use SOD to build world-class products, rapidly and accurately. To get the most out of SOD the designer has to use the product continuously, from day one, and develop his or her ability to smell out problems such as inconsistency, surprising behavior, and other forms of friction. We naturally overlook many annoyances, but a good designer picks these up and thinks about how to patch them. Design is about removing friction in the use of a product.

In an open source setting, we do this work in public. There's no "let's open the code" moment. Projects that do this are in my view missing the point of open source, which is to engage your users in your exploration, and to build community around the seed of the architecture.

Burnout

The ZeroMQ community has been and still is heavily dependent on pro bono individual efforts. I'd like to think that everyone was compensated in some way for their contributions, and I believe that with ZeroMQ, contributing means gaining expertise in an extraordinarily valuable technology, which leads to improved professional options.

However, not all projects will be so lucky and if you work with or in open source, you should understand the risk of burnout that volunteers face. This applies to all pro bono communities. In this section, I'll explain what causes burnout, how to recognize it, how to prevent it, and (if it happens) how to try to treat it. Disclaimer: I'm not a psychiatrist and this article is based on my own experiences of working in pro bono contexts for the last 20 years, including free software projects, and NGOs such as the FFII[29].

In a pro bono context, we're expected to work without direct or obvious economic incentive. That is, we sacrifice family life, professional advancement, free time, and health in order to accomplish some goal we have decided to accomplish. In any project, we need some kind of reward to make it worth continuing each day. In most pro bono projects the rewards are very indirect, superficially not economical at all. Mostly, we do things because people say, "Hey, great!" Karma is a powerful motivator.

However, we are economic beings, and sooner or later, if a project costs us a great deal and does not bring economic rewards of some kind (money, fame, a new job), we start to suffer. At a certain stage, it seems our subconscious simply gets disgusted and says, "Enough is enough!" and refuses to go any further. If we try to force ourselves, we can literally get sick.

This is what I call "burnout", though the term is also used for other kinds of exhaustion. Too much investment on a project with too little

---

29   http://www.ffii.org

economic reward, for too long. We are great at manipulating ourselves and others, and this is often part of the process that leads to burnout. We tell ourselves that it's for a good cause and that the other guy is doing OK, so we should be able to as well.

When I got burned out on open source projects like Xitami, I remember clearly how I felt. I simply stopped working on it, refused to answer any more emails, and told people to forget about it. You can tell when someone's burned out. They go offline, and everyone starts saying, "He's acting strange... depressed, or tired..."

Diagnosis is simple. Has someone worked a lot on a project that was not paying back in any way? Did she make exceptional sacrifices? Did he lose or abandon his job or studies to do the project? If you're answering "yes", it's burnout.

There are three simple techniques I've developed over the years to reduce the risk of burnout in the teams I work with:

- *No one is irreplaceable.* Working solo on a critical or popular project—the concentration of responsibility on one person who cannot set their own limits—is probably the main factor. It's a management truism: if someone in your organization is irreplaceable, get rid of him or her.

- *We need day jobs to pay the bills.* This can be hard, but seems necessary. Getting money from somewhere else makes it much easier to sustain a sacrificial project.

- *Teach people about burnout.* This should be a basic course in colleges and universities, as pro bono work becomes a more common way for young people to experiment professionally.

When someone is working alone on a critical project, you *know* they are going blow their fuses sooner or later. It's actually fairly predictable: something like 18-36 months depending on the individual and how much economic stress they face in their private lives. I've not seen anyone burn-out after half a year, nor last five years in a unrewarding project.

There is a simple cure for burnout that works in at least some cases: get paid decently for your work. However, this pretty much destroys the freedom of movement (across that infinite problem landscape) that the volunteer enjoys.

Patterns for Success

I'll end this code-free chapter with a series of patterns for success in software engineering. They aim to capture the essence of what divides glorious success from tragic failure. They were described as "religious maniacal dogma" by a manager, and "anything else would be effing insane" by a colleague, in a single day. For me, they are science. But treat the Lazy Perfectionist and others as tools to use, sharpen, and throw away if something better comes along.

The Lazy Perfectionist

Never design anything that's not a precise minimal answer to a problem we can identify and have to solve.

The Lazy Perfectionist spends his idle time observing others and identifying problems that are worth solving. He looks for agreement on those problems, always asking, "What is the *real* problem". Then he moves, precisely and minimally, to build, or get others to build, a usable answer to one problem. He uses, or gets others to use those solutions. And he repeats this until there are no problems left to solve, or time or money runs out.

The Benevolent Tyrant

The control of a large force is the same principle as the control of a few men: it is merely a question of dividing up their numbers. — Sun Tzu

The Benevolent Tyrant divides large problems into smaller ones and throws them at groups to focus on. She brokers contracts between these groups, in the form of APIs and the "unprotocols" we'll read about in the next chapter. The Benevolent Tyrant constructs a supply chain that starts with problems, and results in usable solutions. She is ruthless about how the supply chain works, but does not tell people what to work on, nor how to do their work.

The Earth and Sky

The ideal team consists of two sides: one writing code, and one providing feedback.

The Earth and Sky work together as a whole, in close proximity, but they communicate formally through issue tracking. Sky seeks out problems from others and from their own use of the product and feeds these to Earth. Earth rapidly answers with testable solutions. Earth and Sky can work through dozens of issues in a day. Sky talks to other users, and Earth talks to other developers. Earth and Sky may be two people, or two small groups.

The Open Door

The accuracy of knowledge comes from diversity.

The Open Door accepts contributions from almost anyone. She does not argue quality or direction, instead allowing others to argue that and get more engaged. She calculates that even a troll will bring more diverse opinion to the group. She lets the group form its opinion about what goes into stable code, and she enforces this opinion with help of a Benevolent Tyrant.

The Laughing Clown

Perfection precludes participation.

The Laughing Clown, often acting as the Happy Failure, makes no claim to high competence. Instead his antics and bumbling attempts provoke others into rescuing him from his own tragedy. Somehow however, he always identifies the right problems to solve. People are so busy proving him wrong they don't realize they're doing valuable work.

The Mindful General

Make no plans. Set goals, develop strategies and tactics.

The Mindful General operates in unknown territory, solving problems that are hidden until they are nearby. Thus she makes no plans, but seeks opportunities, then exploits them rapidly and accurately. She develops tactics and strategies in the field, and teaches these to her soldiers so they can move independently, and together.

The Social Engineer

If you know the enemy and know yourself, you need not fear the result of a hundred battles. — Sun Tzu

The Social Engineer reads the hearts and minds of those he works with and for. He asks, of everyone, "What makes this person angry, insecure, argumentative, calm, happy?" He studies their moods and dispositions. With this knowledge he can encourage those who are useful, and discourage those who are not. The Social Engineer never acts on his own emotions.

The Constant Gardener

He will win whose army is animated by the same spirit throughout all its ranks. — Sun Tzu

The Constant Gardener grows a process from a small seed, step-by-step as more people come into the project. She makes every change for a precise reason, with agreement from everyone. She never imposes a process from above but lets others come to consensus, and then he enforces that consensus. In this way, everyone owns the process together and by owning it, they are attached to it.

The Rolling Stone

After crossing a river, you should get far away from it. — Sun Tzu

The Rolling Stone accepts his own mortality and transience. He has no attachment to his past work. He accepts that all that we make is destined for the trash can, it is just a matter of time. With precise, minimal investments, he can move rapidly away from the past and stay focused on the present and near future. Above all, he has no ego and no pride to be hurt by the actions of others.

The Pirate Gang

Code, like all knowledge, works best as collective—not private—property.

The Pirate Gang organizes freely around problems. It accepts authority insofar as authority provides goals and resources. The Pirate Gang owns and shares all it makes: every work is fully remixable by others in the Pirate Gang. The gang moves rapidly as new problems emerge, and is quick to abandon old solutions if those stop being relevant. No persons or groups can monopolize any part of the supply chain.

The Flash Mob

Water shapes its course according to the nature of the ground over which it flows. — Sun Tzu

The Flash Mob comes together in space and time as needed, then disperses as soon as they can. Physical closeness is essential for high-bandwidth communications. But over time it creates technical ghettos, where Earth gets separated from Sky. The Flash Mob tends to collect a lot of frequent flier miles.

The Canary Watcher

Pain is not, generally, a Good Sign.

The Canary Watcher measures the quality of an organization by their own pain level, and the observed pain levels of those with whom he works. He brings new participants into existing organizations so they can express the raw pain of the innocent. He may use alcohol to get others to verbalize their pain points. He asks others, and himself, "Are you happy in this process, and if not, why not?" When an organization causes pain in himself or others, he treats that as a problem to be fixed. People should feel joy in their work.

The Hangman

Never interrupt others when they are making mistakes.

The Hangman knows that we learn only by making mistakes, and she gives others copious rope with which to learn. She only pulls the rope gently, when it's time. A little tug to remind the other of their precarious position. Allowing others to learn by failure gives the good reason to stay, and the bad excuse to leave. The Hangman is endlessly patient, because there is no shortcut to the learning process.

The Historian

Keeping the public record may be tedious, but it's the only way to prevent collusion.

The Historian forces discussion into the public view, to prevent collusion to own areas of work. The Pirate Gang depends on full and equal communications that do not depend on momentary presence. No one really reads the archives, but the simply possibility stops most abuses. The Historian encourages the right tool for the job: email for transient discussions, IRC for chatter, wikis for knowledge, issue tracking for recording opportunities.

The Provocateur

When a man knows he is to be hanged in a fortnight, it concentrates his mind wonderfully. — Samuel Johnson

The Provocateur creates deadlines, enemies, and the occasional impossibility. Teams work best when they don't have time for the crap. Deadlines bring people together and focus the collective mind. An external enemy can move a passive team into action. The Provocateur never takes the deadline too seriously. The product is *always* ready to ship. But she gently reminds the team of the stakes: fail, and we all look for other jobs.

The Mystic

When people argue or complain, just write them a Sun Tzu quotation — Mikko Koppanen

The Mystic never argues directly. He knows that to argue with an emotional person only creates more emotion. Instead he side-steps the discussion. It's hard to be angry at a Chinese general, especially when he has been dead for 2,400 years. The Mystic plays Hangman when people insist on the right to get it wrong.

Chapter 6. Living Systems

A "Living System" is one that grows into its environment, by self-organizing around opportunities. Living systems can last for a long time, adapt well to change, and thus be highly successful. By contrast, "Planned Systems" tend to be fragile, poor at coping with change, and thus short-lived. In this article I'll explain Living Systems, of software and people, and how to grow them.

Why "Living Systems"?

Since the beginning, life has relied upon the transmission of messages. — RFC 3164 (syslog)[30]

Wikipedia writes[31], "Living systems are open self-organizing living things that interact with their environment. These systems are maintained by flows of information, energy and matter." The term was originated by psychologist James Grier Miller to formalize the concept of life.

I want to use the term to define a new metaphor for software systems and organizations, the two types of system I'm most interested in. The two are more than just similar. Software is the product of an group of people, and as Conway observed, the structure of a software system mimics the structure of the organization that produces it. I've written that "the physics of software is the physics of people," and by that I meant psychology.

Most software products today are highly planned, and they fail as living systems. They are essentially dead on delivery, sold by force and bluff. For a software to be a "living system", it must be used by the organization that builds it, and it then lives or dies along with that organization. An "organization" can be much larger than one company

---

30 http://www.ietf.org/rfc/rfc3164.txt
31 http://en.wikipedia.org/wiki/Living_systems

or one team. It can consist of thousands of teams, businesses, customers and suppliers, connected in ineffable yet vitally real networks.

Nowhere is this more clear than the Internet, a Living System of software, of people, of businesses and other organizations. The organization that built the Internet is nothing less than human society itself. There are many Living Systems, all around us. It is a strangely simple truth: that the better we get at writing large-scale software systems, they more they resemble the real world around us.

In contrast to Living Systems, we have Planned Systems. It is far easier to plan a system than to grow it. However, plans are inevitably built on wrong assumptions and poor judgments. Planned Systems look attractive and efficient from some perspectives, yet they inevitably fail catastrophically. Real life provides many examples, such as collective farming, planned cities, Microsoft Windows 8, and so on.

In the software business, this Living vs. Planned dichotomy is best expressed by free software vs. closed source. Free software (and its corporate cousin open source) usually grows out of real use, where as closed source is usually planned. This is mainly why I don't work on closed source: it dies rapidly and predictably. I prefer my work to survive as long as possible.

I'll make a few broad claims, starting with: *the most successful large-scale software systems are Living Systems.* That is, in a competitive market, a Living System will wipe out any competing Planned Systems. It will recognize and solve real problems faster, cheaper, and more accurately. If your business depends on a Planned System, you are vulnerable to attack by a Living System.

The second claim I'll make is that this also applies to organizations. If your company is a Planned System, it is already dead. Whereas if your company operates as a Living System, it can dominate its market. Interestingly, when two Living Systems meet, they don't usually fight. Rather, they specialize into different areas, and they then merge to form a single Living System. Competition and conflict usually work for the benefit of the Living System, even if individual components fail.

Let me take this question of conflict and competition further. Of course individuals do compete, and quite harshly sometimes. This is our biological imperative. However we also have a biological imperative to collaborate, a far more profitable strategy, most of the time. A Living System embraces competition between individuals, and survives the failure of individual components. It actually depends on that process of competition and failure. A Planned System is essentially trying to act as a single individual, and cannot tolerate internal competition, nor failure of individual components.

What do Living Systems Look Like?

A Living System consists of a large number of loosely-coupled components. It is essentially spread out in space (thus, "distributed"), and in time (thus, "asynchronous"). That means things happen in unpredictable places, and at unexpected times. To a central planner, this looks like dangerous chaos.

In a Planned System, by contrast, the times and places of events are meticulously scripted. The focus is on "command and control," where decisions are made centrally and communicated to the structure. Planned Systems are essentially hierarchical, for this is the optimum way to communicate decisions rapidly down from the top.

We *build* a Planned System, whereas a Living System *grows* itself. My goal is to learn, and to teach, how to grow Living Systems artificially. I'm studying the genes and patterns of care and nurture for a self-growing system. In fact I'm talking about creating artificial life, and artificial intelligence, though in a shape that traditional AI researchers might not recognize. I don't believe individuals components — including you and me — can be "intelligent" at all, except in a narrow and superficial sense: intelligence is a property of systems.

Living Systems are typified by their lack of central planning or decision making. Look at a software project and ask, "who is the designer?" If there is a clear designer, individual or organization (and there almost always is), that is a Planned System. A Living System has no designer, no road-maps, no clear future plans except "survive and grow."

A Living System looks more like Adam Smith's free market than Stalin's Five Year Plan. Economics, politics, and psychology are as important — perhaps more important — in growing successful Living Systems as technology. A free market depends on several key things: clear laws, standards, contracts, and fair regulation. A Living System likewise depends on these.

So whereas a Living System has no central planner, it may have central regulators. Let me explain the difference. In a planned city, a committee decides where to build schools, homes, factories, offices, railway stations, shops, sports facilities, and so on. In a Living City, all these are decided by independent agents (school boards, businesses, home owners, etc.) and the city regulates the provision of electricity and clean water, the disposal of garbage, and so on. Further, the city runs police and courts, as regulators, to dissuade criminals and cheats.

A regulator makes laws that define a fair market, and then enforces those laws. Units of measurement, currencies, contracts, and such. In software systems, these laws are, for instance, the source code license, and contribution policy. A fair market lets anyone create a new venture, and compete with other ventures. To allow true competition (meaning, free choice by customers), clients can demand clear contracts, which in software terms are documented APIs and protocols.

The DNA of a Living Systems is essentially a set of regulated contracts. Thus the Internet is grown out of a set of RFCs (protocols called Requests for Comments), regulated by the Internet Engineering Task Force (IETF). Living cities are grown out of criminal and civil laws, standards for water and power and waste, transport, and so on.

If all strategies were honest, there would be no need for regulators. However any Living System will be vulnerable to cheating strategies.

A certain segment of people, for instance, are systematic or opportunistic cheats. Given a market, they will always seek a way to convert value to their own benefit, even at a higher cost to others. They will lie, steal, deceive, coerce, and so on.

Without resistance against such cheats, the market will suffer, and the system will eventually die. Top-down authority is one defense against cheats. However it has a significant vulnerability: cheats can, and often do, capture the authority itself. In Living Systems, cheats can try to capture the regulators, and this happens in real life all the time.

When cheats capture the regulators of real-life Living Systems, the usual response is to move away, if we can. In open source software systems, we can fork and continue under a better regulator. This is why forking is an essential freedom, rather than a failure. Since forking can also be a strategy for capture, a fork-safe license (GPL or similar) is best for Living Systems in software.

Living Systems grow, constantly and organically. This is their most visible trait: the lack of the usual massive construction efforts. Rather, you will see a smooth flow of small changes. It may seem boring or unambitious. However, it is a better algorithm for survival. A Living System must do two things. First, it must solve some profitable set of problems. Second, it must adapt and change over time, as its environment changes.

Shifting a Planned System to cope with a changing environment is very hard, often impossible. Resources define power. Thus, Planned Systems actively and aggressively resist change, deny it, and when it becomes inevitable, they die catastrophically. However, a Living System feeds off change. It makes no distinction between exploring the landscape of problems of "now" and of "tomorrow." It grows through continuous learning. To actually destroy a Living System you have to do widespread damage to it, which is hard when a successful Living System has spread wide.

To a Living System, small amounts of damage are indistinguishable from normal activity. In fact Living Systems thrive on challenge, so long as it is not overwhelming. Challenge is what allows components to compete, and develop better answers. What does not kill a Living System makes it stronger.

So, as Living Systems learn and move quickly and opportunistically into new areas, they will tend to thrive and grow dominant, wiping out any competing Planned Systems. They can react rapidly, shifting resources around to areas where they are more valuable. And since they do not need any upfront coordination to act, they can scale to any size. Zero upfront coordination means infinite scale.

Components of a Living System

Let's now look at the individual components of a Living System. Remember that a Living System resembles a free market, where components compete to provide some identifiable and measurable service. The components of a Living System have some traits that set them apart from the components of a planned system.

Every component of a Living System has a clear set of owners and investors, and ownership is usually highly localized (in contrast to a Planned System, where all components have the same owners). Components organize into chains of suppliers and clients, and they have identities, names, and addresses, so that clients can find them. One classic way to cheat is for one group to provide a poor quality component that claims to be a high-quality one. Thus the regulator may have to enforce identity, and protect investment in an identity.

Components are, as far as possible, location independent. That creates a larger, and more efficient free market. It means that we strive for location independence as a feature of our Living System. This is contrary to a Planned System, where location is highly significant, and where there is little or no competition between components.

Similarly, components may come and go in time, quite arbitrarily. There are no guarantees that a component we depend on today will still exist, or be available tomorrow. This may sound fragile, yet it is highly robust. Rather than depending on specific components, we depend on contracts. If our need is real, there will be many alternatives. If one disappears, another will take its place. If you miss one taxi, you will catch another.

Components are highly independent, decoupled from one another. That is, they exist and change at their own rate, in their own direction. A change in one component is essentially invisible to another component except through its public interfaces. This freedom is essential to a free market, driven by specialization and trade. Thus one component may focus on speed, while another on security.

Since there is no centralized decision about what components exist, nor who makes them, they will be highly heterogeneous, and this diversity is essential to the intelligence of the overall system. A set of diverse components in a Living System, connected in a free market, will solve large problems faster, and more accurately, than a monolithic Planned System.

Components are abstracted, meaning they may represent entire systems in themselves. For instance a web address can represent a single, small piece of software (one web server), or it may represent a massive infrastructure (an Internet business). It is up to each group of owners to decide whether they build Living Systems or Planned Systems, in turn. A Living System will happily embrace Planned Systems as components. The opposite isn't true.

Components avoid upfront consensus, also known as "shared mutable state". Every component has knowledge, and they may share knowledge, yet they do so asynchronously. So while the Living System represents a large, coherent pool of knowledge, there is no guaranteed consistency between components. This may seem paradoxical. Surely every person in a meeting, for instance, agrees on the agenda for the meeting?

In fact meetings, with their agendas and minutes, are the epitome of the shared mutable state that a Planned System depends on.

Planned Systems cannot function without systematic upfront agreement. In concurrent software design, we use "locks" to achieve the same result. It is provably true that a software system that uses locks to share state between components will not scale. You can try to make distributed software as a Planned System: it starts easily yet scales poorly, if at all. Whereas a Living System takes a little more thought at the start, and then scales without limit.

Finally, components are lazy and opportunistic. They only work when there are tasks waiting, and they only change and grow when there are new, profitable opportunities. This means components can remain lightweight and minimalistic. Further, they can solve the "problem landscape" much more accurately, without excess baggage. In a Planned System by contrast, components are built upfront, on the assumption of future problems, or at best, knowledge of past problems.

An example: in a planned conference, the organizers choose speakers on certain topics, based on their experience of the previous year. Now, one month before the conference, a significant event drives public demand for speakers on a totally different topic. How long will it take the conference to react? A participant-driven conference can react in real-time, whereas a planned conference will take a full year to respond.

Protocols of a Living System

The components of a Living System are connected in relationships. Each relationship consists of a flow of information, knowledge, or requests, in both directions. The best way to model such relationship seems to be as discrete events, or "messages," that carry a formalized set of interactions we call "protocols."

In natural Living Systems, we also see messages and protocols. Cells, for instance, communicate with chemical messages. We humans appear to communicate with a set of protocols that underly our human languages. For instance, male-dominated hierarchies are a consistent feature of human society, suggesting that the command-and-control protocols they depend on are built-in to our minds, not learned. I'd hypothesize that the male mind, driven by the ancestral need to plan hunting parties, is responsible for Planned Systems.

Protocols have a number of common patterns. We see broadcast protocols where one component signals to many listeners. A broadcast protocol is typically one-way. The signaler may, in rare occasions, get feedback from a few listeners.

We see one-to-one protocols where two components exchange knowledge, tasks, requests, and so on. One-to-one protocols can be more or less chatty, and ideally are fully asynchronous. Chattier protocols take longer to conclude, thus raising overall "latency." For example if I'm cooking a pizza and I have to confirm every ingredient, it will take longer. "Do you like mushrooms?" "How about garlic?" "Ok, what kind of cheese do you prefer?"

The ideal relationships aim for lowest realistic latency, since the latency of the overall system is the sum of the latency of its entire supply chain. That is, if I'm making a meal, and I have to spend one minute solving the "pizza" issue, that adds one minute to the overall preparation time. In an asynchronous low-latency dialog, I'd ask all the questions at once, and deal with the answers as I got them back, one by one.

To make effective asynchronous systems we need queues, and smart queuing strategies. Ideally, we have queues at any point where messages may arrive, and we push messages as close to their consumers as possible, to reduce latency. We need strategies to deal with full queues (space is not infinite): it might be to throw away older messages, or to pause the sender (this works for one-to-one dialogs, not for one-to-many). We may need multiple incoming queues, one per flow, and the ability to wait for a message on any of these queues.

The protocols of a Living System are highly ritualized. They implement formal contracts. If I ask, "Do you like garlic?" then I expect a yes/no answer. A discussion about the weather is a breach of contract.

When we're growing our own Living Systems, we have to write the protocols down, so they can be learned and verified. The simpler and clearer, the better. Complex, arcane protocols are expensive to learn and implement, which distorts the free market.

Some Living Systems use earned trust, together with identity, in place of verifiable contracts. This can be a valuable short-hand, especially when exchanging knowledge, though it is also vulnerable to cheats (frauds). An alternative is to ensure that every contract is verifiable, backed by meta-contracts on performance. This is often better for trading work. Any taxi driver is fine, so long as drive to the right address and don't over-charge. However we want our news from trusted sources.

Once we have testable contracts we can deal with violations. One strategy is to fail, and let someone else deal with it. Another is to discard that peer and try another. However, after a contract violation, you generally don't want to continue blindly, as that can cause wider damage.

Case Study: the ZeroMQ Community

The ZeroMQ community is a Living System of people that builds a Living System of software (the software collection under the same name). Though I originally designed the ZeroMQ community with most of the properties of a Living System, it only really came true in early 2012, when the community rejected its central planners.

The community consists of a large number of loosely-coupled projects that share a common goal, which is to provide the queuing and messaging needs for other software systems. I've argued, and believe, that only a Living System can use ZeroMQ optimally.

The ZeroMQ projects are connected into a supply chain by formalized relationships, over APIs and wire protocols. We spend a large amount of time documenting these APIs and protocols, and ensuring they are testable. Indeed, we do not usually document the internals of components, just their external APIs.

There is no central planning nor coordination. Instead, each project evolves organically as its users invest in patches and improvements. By making this process simple, the ZeroMQ collaboration contract[32] ensures that the ZeroMQ organization expands to include all its competent users.

Anyone can start a new ZeroMQ project, or fork an existing one, for competition or experimentation. As a community we encourage this, and so we have multiple competitors at most levels. This works well in practice. The basic license is LGPL v3 or MPL v2, ensuring that forks are always safe (patches can flow in both directions).

The regulator in the ZeroMQ community is a self-elected group, headed by iMatix, the firm that developed the original software. There is not much regulation needed, except to stop abuse of the name "ZeroMQ". Clear documentation of protocols is sufficient to allow clients to verify their suppliers.

ZeroMQ is highly scalable. The cost of adding a new project is close to zero, apart from the discovery cost. Projects communicate asynchronously, using GitHub issues and pull requests. There is little or no upfront coordination. We review code after the fact, and fix poor code through further patches rather than discussion.

ZeroMQ's full transition to a Living System was hard because we had no prior successes to imitate. The bulk of free software projects still depend on significant planning. To go against standard practice was seen as highly eccentric, if not actually insane. The loss of key contributors — who had provided the authority that central planning depends on — was seen as potentially catastrophic.

However the ZeroMQ community rapidly expanded into the space left by the central planners, and flourished. We disproved the theory that central planning was essential to quality. In fact we found that without central planning, the software improved significantly in quality and in accuracy. Whereas the ZeroMQ development branch had

---

32   http://rfc.zeromq.org/spec:22

been highly unstable, experimental, and discordant with users' needs, it became mostly stable, trusted, and a close fit for users' needs.

Today we can hold the ZeroMQ community as a worked example of how to do Living Systems "right." It is all the more valuable as data since there have been numerous attempts to replace it, both by the fleeing central planners, and by other teams. Noticeably, every Planned System that claimed to be "better than ZeroMQ" has failed, whereas every Living System that began by competing with ZeroMQ ended up becoming a valuable part of it.

Transforming into a Living System

Can we turn a Planned System into a Living System? If we assume we have the technical right (consensus from enough participants, or legal right through software licensing), what are the practical require-ments?

The most difficult part will be to get the size of components right. This will often mean breaking up existing components, and creating new ones. That can be catastrophic if done in too many places at once. Thus, in a larger migration, you would start in one area, refactor that, and then grow the resulting culture out.

Components are usually sized around the people, so a good size is "the work that a few people can do." The scale of a Living System comes from adding more components, and allowing them to use and replace each other in whatever fashion makes sense locally, not in-creasing individual component size. A component is too small when it cannot provide a full service by itself, and it is too large when it does not focus on one thing.

Finally, you need the contracts. For a software system, we have had good results simply by taking the the ZeroMQ C4.1 process contract[33], and using that together with a code style guide and the software li-cense. For several reasons, I strongly recommend a share-alike license,

---

33   http://rfc.zeromq.org/spec:22

such as LGPL (my thesis is that if you use a leaky license like Apache or BSD, you in fact won't get a successful Living System at all).

Launching such a Living System in the past was difficult, as self-organizing software ecologies were poorly documented and little understood. We lacked empirical evidence that processes like C4.1 could work, let alone work so well. As far as I know, this was the first documented contract for a Living System in software.

Economics of Living Systems

How do we make money from free software? It is a question I'm often asked. The answer comes in various forms depending on whether I'm talking to individuals, to small firms, or to large firms.

A key understanding of Living Systems is that they are essentially about economics. No component exists for random reasons. However, to offer a choice between selfishness and altruism is a false dichotomy. Living Systems are driven by selfishness and altruism at the same time. It is a basic theory of economics: by selfish specialization and trade, we create common wealth. It is the human species' superpower: specialization and trade at a massive scale, between individuals, families, generations, villages, cities, and entire regions.

A Living System is owned by all participants, so it can be harder to measure its value, whereas a Planned System, owned by a few at the top, can have very visible value, to its owners and outside observers. However the overall value and economic power of a Living System will always overwhelm any competing Planned System. A Living System can be incredibly profitable, its profits are just widely distributed among all its participants.

This is the first answer: a Living System can kill competing Planned Systems, and thus liberate large amounts of captive value, which can be absorbed by the Living System. We see this in real life, where free market economies out-perform planned economies, leading to movement of skilled labor (value) from the latter to the former.

The second answer is that we can build new markets on top of successful Living Systems, that are impossible on Planned Systems. The Internet is a clear example of this: it has enabled a massive new economy that was impossible on older networks. Those new markets can be very profitable.

A Planned System can only survive by taking value away from its components. In many ways, it resembles a cult, and depends on cult techniques like brain washing, where a few prosper at the expense of many. Planned Systems are inherently unethical, as well as unsustainable. There is an inherent morality in a fair and free market, despite the large number of of Planned Systems that claim to represent "the market."

Conclusions

In this essay I've looked at artificial Living Systems, which imitate and can be modeled on real living systems. Living Systems are spread out in space and time. They consist of large numbers of independently owned components that work together, competing and collaborating, in a free market for services, labor, resources, and knowledge. These components evolve independently, under pressure from their market. They live and die according to their success in finding accurate answers to real problems faced by their clients.

The components in a Living System communicate asynchronously by passing messages around, in various patterns. These flows are highly ritualized, in the form of protocols. The more accurate the protocol, the easier it is for clients to choose suppliers freely, and the more efficient the market.

A Living System has no central controlling owner, though it may elect authorities to regulate (define, and enforce) contracts. It has no single points of failure. Rather than treating failure as exceptional and to be avoided, it uses failure as a basic learning technique. Inaccurate components are allowed to fail and are discarded rapidly, and replaced by more accurate components.

Living Systems grow by learning, into supply chains that connect components to the external environment. We can measure the efficiency of a Living System by looking at overall latency as a problem enters the system, and a response emerges. Such latencies can vary from years in Planned Systems to hours in highly adaptive Living Systems.

Living Systems thus organize opportunistically, accurately judging the relative cost of a given problem, and the value of solving it. Unlike Planned Systems, they are driven by live data rather than assumptions, beliefs, or old data. This lets them operate more accurately, faster, and cheaper than Planned Systems.

To build a large scale Living System in software, build a Living System of people. The two will co-evolve and done correctly, will dominate any given market. Whereas competing Planned Systems will fail as whole units, competing Living Systems will tend to specialize into different areas, and then merge into a single unified Living System.

Postface

This book tells a long story that started when I read Stallman's accounts of writing his first free software. In 2005 we were building online communities deliberately and aggressively, for political purposes. By then we'd codified the theory and were applying it over and over. In 2007 I used this to build a large community for the Wikidot.com platform, which I'd invested in and was CEO of. In 2009 I used it as the basis for the ZeroMQ community, and by 2011 had turned this fire on full, stripping away all the old clumsy patterns, and replacing them with upgraded state-of-the-art techniques.

We are still learning, making our processes simpler, and our tools sharper. C4 is not for everyone. It takes courage to embrace unknown contributors and trust them by default. It takes experience to realize that for every twenty smiles, there is one knife. We learn these lessons slowly. Even with a full handbook, it will take you years to understand. So practice, be prepared to fail often, and be happy. :)

Printed in Great Britain
by Amazon

29146988R00077